Frank Lloyd Wright *and* MASON CITY

Frank Lloyd Wright *and* MASON CITY

ARCHITECTURAL HEART OF THE PRAIRIE

ROY R. BEHRENS

FOREWORD BY ANN ELIAS

THE History PRESS

Published by The History Press
Charleston, SC
www.historypress.net

First published 2016

Manufactured in the United States

ISBN 978.1.46711.860.6

Library of Congress Control Number: 2016947478

In memory of Merle Armitage (1893–1975), who was born in Mason City. A friend of Frank Lloyd Wright, he went on to become the art director of Look *magazine and one of the most innovative book designers of the twentieth century.*

High above the prairie, platter-flat, the wind wings on, bereft and wild its lonely song.
—W.O. Mitchell

We have left less than one-tenth of one percent of our prairie. The rest of it died to make Iowa safe for soybeans.
—Loren Lown

[The Rock Crest/Rock Glen neighborhood in Mason City, Iowa, is] *the most successfully realized Prairie School development anywhere in America.*
—Alasdair McGregor

CONTENTS

FOREWORD

There is an ornamental lake in the center of the city of Canberra, the federal capital of Australia: Lake Burley Griffin. It was named to commemorate the American architect and urban planner Walter Burley Griffin, who in 1912, with his collaborator and wife, Marion Mahony, won an international competition to design the nation's future capital city. As Burley Griffin later emphasized, his plan for Canberra was for an ideal city where the beauty of nature and the needs of community would be met in the harmony of landscape and town planning. It was the Prairie School philosophy brought to the Antipodes, an approach to urban design and architecture associated with the Griffins but also Frank Lloyd Wright. Unfortunately, the Canberra commission ended badly, with Griffin protesting in national newspapers a breach of faith. He eventually departed Australian shores, but not before leaving an indelible impression on Australian culture by raising the appreciation of native flora and redesigning parts of the city of Sydney, including the suburb of Castlecrag, where his philosophy was to integrate houses with native trees and local sandstone landforms.

The story of the Griffins in Australia involves vast physical distances traveled and vast cultural distances encountered, especially their experience of the gap between progressives and traditionalists. A parallel story is told here in this revelational book by Roy Behrens of how Walter Burley Griffin, Marion Mahony and their more famous associate Frank Lloyd Wright also bridged the cultural divide between the metropolis and margins to bring modernism to Mason City, Iowa. The triumphs, battles and disappointments of these visionary architects are a large part of the story that unfolds under the analytical and often witty pen of the author. Readers will learn how, from 1908 to 1912, the Griffins and Frank Lloyd Wright left the mark of the Prairie School on a bank, a hotel and a neighborhood and how, in order for Griffin to accept the Canberra commission, he had to leave in abeyance the design of a neighborhood of houses in Mason City known as Rock Crest/ Rock Glen.

In this book, the author deftly weaves the various threads that make up the remarkable story of how America's great architects enriched the aesthetics and social life of Mason City. He reveals a palimpsest woven of folklore, history, politics and culture. He shows us the context for the architectural languages written over the city by Frank Lloyd Wright, Walter Burley Griffin and Marion Mahony and erased by the foibles of progress, only to be restored and rescued in recent times. For Behrens, though, the restorations are "a breathtaking triumph in building design that reaffirms human achievement."

In this book, the clear and engaging voice of Roy Behrens gives us much more than broad strokes: he intrigues through a historian's fascination with coincidences, events and surprises, and he enlightens with a designer's fascinated eye for space, forms, materials and illusions. Mason City, as told by Behrens, is a passionate story emanating from a scholar who is himself immersed in the landscape and history of Iowa. We reach the end of the book with a sense of the wholeness of history, not dissimilar to the concept of the total work of art that informed the Prairie School.

—Ann Elias

Dr. Ann Elias is associate professor in art theory at Sydney College of the Arts, University of Sydney, Australia. Her research interests include camouflage as a military, social and aesthetic phenomenon; flowers and their cultural history; and coral reef imagery of the underwater realm. Her books include *Camouflage Australia: Art, Nature, Science and War* (University of Sydney Press, 2011); *Useless Beauty: Flowers and Australian Art* (Cambridge Scholars Publishing, 2015); and *Camouflage Cultures: Beyond the Art of Disappearance*, edited by Ann Elias, Ross Harley and Nicholas Tsoutas (Sydney University Press, 2015).

ACKNOWLEDGEMENTS

For more than twenty years, I have taught a university course on the history of modern-era design. Like this account of Mason City architecture, the lectures in that course begin around 1850 and progress toward the present time. The ideas in this book took shape over the years as I was preparing those lectures.

This project required a number of trips to Mason City, about two hours from our farm. My wonderful wife, Mary Synder Behrens, was unwaveringly supportive, as she invariably has been throughout our years of married life.

I also gained considerably from conversations about Frank Lloyd Wright, the Griffins and Prairie School architecture with Robert E. McCoy (an authority on Rock Crest/Rock Glen and owner of the Blythe House) and Peggy Bang (owner of the Melson House), as well as informal exchanges with Iowa friends and Prairie School enthusiasts, among them Geraldine Schwarz (a Mason City native), Paul and Anita Whitson, Rick Knivsland (of the Friends of Cedar Rock) and Richard H. Behrens.

As I searched for photographs, Mary Markwalter (director of the Mason City Public Library) and Terry Harrison (its historian and archivist) were especially helpful. I was also enormously pleased when historian Ann Elias agreed to contribute a foreword, which is an especially suitable way to underscore the link between Mason City and Sydney, Australia. I am also indebted to the editors at The History Press for suggesting that I take this on and for all their diligent work in enabling it to become a reality.

INTRODUCTION

Soon after his arrival in the United States, a young German architect named Richard Neutra was walking through the neighborhoods of the Hyde Park area of Chicago looking for Prairie School houses.[1]

Earlier, in a European library, he had seen the *Wasmuth Portfolio*, an album of early buildings by American architect Frank Lloyd Wright. Now, he had come to Chicago to search for one of Wright's most admired designs: the famous Frederick C. Robie House on Woodlawn Avenue.

Standing at last in the presence of the Robie House, Neutra was infused with emotion. He rang the doorbell and asked in broken English, "Is Mr. Robie in?" The present owner, who answered the door, replied, "Mr. Robie? Never heard of him." There had been a succession of owners, and she had bought the house, she explained, because it was "very cheap" and the previous owner "had to get out." She didn't particularly like its design, Neutra recalled, and "had all kinds of petty criticisms."[2]

In his autobiography, Neutra recalled that this happened repeatedly as he visited famous American buildings, well known and admired by European architects. Inevitably, he found that the current residents (and their neighbors) had little or no understanding of the importance of the buildings that surrounded them. He was overtaken by what he described as a "sad wonderment."

"I had arrived in fairyland," he said, "but the fairies had gone. And the occupants of the enchanted forest looked entirely inconsistent and contradictory to what their setting called for. I was downcast, broken, and puzzled."[3]

Later, when Neutra actually met Frank Lloyd Wright, he told him how surprised he was that Chicago's Prairie School houses were not surrounded by prairie. When those homes were built, he asked, were they then in the prairie?

"No," Wright answered. "There was no prairie...but it was the spirit of the prairie that was recaptured with it and in it."[4]

THIS BOOK IS ABOUT a group of those Prairie School buildings that somehow survived the destruction (if only by the slightest thread) of historic American landmarks in the mid-twentieth century. It is also about a particular midwestern community, since the buildings that it focuses on are all located in or just a few blocks from downtown Mason City, Iowa.[5]

Further, the buildings all have some connection—directly or indirectly—to Frank Lloyd Wright. And in fact, all of them were designed by Wright or his associates.

Mason City is not and never has been an enchanted forest. It is an unpretentious regional hub for agriculture and industry (building materials, meatpacking, food processing) that slumbers in the vast surround of the midwestern prairie. There have been times in the city's past when its architectural treasures have come close to being destroyed. There have also been times when its residents were insufficiently aware and less than appreciative of the historic icons in their midst. But surely the same could be said of nearly any community.

In the case of Mason City, unlike so many American towns, the story has taken a turn for the best. In the 1970s, encouraged by changes in values that enabled the establishment of the National Register of Historic Places, gregarious volunteer citizens' groups (supported and assisted by architectural scholars) began an ongoing campaign to preserve, restore and celebrate the city's historic architecture. That initiative and the generous vision that fueled it are still alive and well today.

These extraordinary efforts have so far resulted in the restoration of Frank Lloyd Wright's Stockman House (now a house museum) and his City National Bank and Park Inn, where guests can once again stay overnight in what is officially known as The Historic Park Inn Hotel. They have also provided construction, in 2011, of the Robert E. McCoy Architectural Interpretive Center, adjacent to the Stockman House. This educational command post dispenses information about the city's architectural heritage through talks, tours and publications.[6]

It is especially helpful that the McCoy Interpretive Center provides an annotated guidebook that vicariously leads its visitors on a self-directed walking tour through the Rock Crest/Rock Glen neighborhood, a cluster of Prairie School houses in a scenic landscape setting that was planned by architect Walter Burley Griffin.

In the process of that neighborhood tour, visitors also discover that Mason City's architectural heritage is far more varied and plentiful than just the Prairie School tradition. As confirmed by such informative texts as *Mason City, An Architectural Heritage*;[7] *Buildings of Iowa*;[8] and *Mason City: Walking Tour Guide*,[9] the city's buildings represent the widest range of architectural monuments.

A sampling of its styles include Streamline Moderne, Art Deco, Richardson Romanesque, Colonial Revival, English Georgian, Craftsman Bungalow, Usonian, Mission Revival, Italian Romanesque, Neoclassical Revival, Queen Anne, Tudor Revival, Shingle Style, International Style, Italianate, Chicago Style and others.[10]

This book is not intended to be a pictorial showcase—that has been more than amply achieved by other recent publications on the subject, books that readers are urged to explore. Instead, it is the story of Mason City and Prairie School architecture in the context of modern-era design. To that end, I have made a particular effort to point out what may be surprising connections between Mason City and the world at large.

"FORM FOLLOWS FUNCTION," as Wright's teacher Louis H. Sullivan liked to say.[11] But perhaps it would be better to note that form and function are inseparable—simply, that "form functions"—and the extent to which it functions well is fundamental to the enduring value of any design, regardless of whether the subject at hand is architectural, graphic, product design or whatever.[12]

"Everything that man makes is designed," design advocate Terence Conran has said, "but not everything is well designed. Good design only comes about when things are made with attention both to their functional and their aesthetic qualities."[13]

Mason City architecture has an abundance of Modernist building designs. How that came about will always be partly a puzzle. And how those remaining buildings escaped demolition—how they not only survived but also flourished at times—is in some measure mysterious, too. I like to think it has to do with the better angels of our nature (in

Lincoln's words) and our need to discover significance in our everyday lives and surroundings.

As Conran went on to say, "Good design starts from the premise that living is more than just a matter of existing, and that everyday things which are both effective and attractive can raise the quality of life."[14]

1

MASON CITY, KINDERGARTEN AND THE IMPERIAL HOTEL

On the first day of September 1923, an American businessman named Walter Scott Rooney (the father of CBS news commentator Andy Rooney) was in his room at the new Imperial Hotel in downtown Tokyo, Japan.[15]

The hotel had been designed by American architect Frank Lloyd Wright, and this was its formal opening day. At two minutes before noon, as Rooney was sitting at a table enjoying a cup of tea, the building suddenly started to shake so violently that the tea spilled out.

In the moments that followed, Tokyo was ripped apart by a massive earthquake, followed by aftershocks, fires and turbulent winds. It was one of the largest, most catastrophic earthquakes in modern history, resulting in as many as 150,000 deaths.

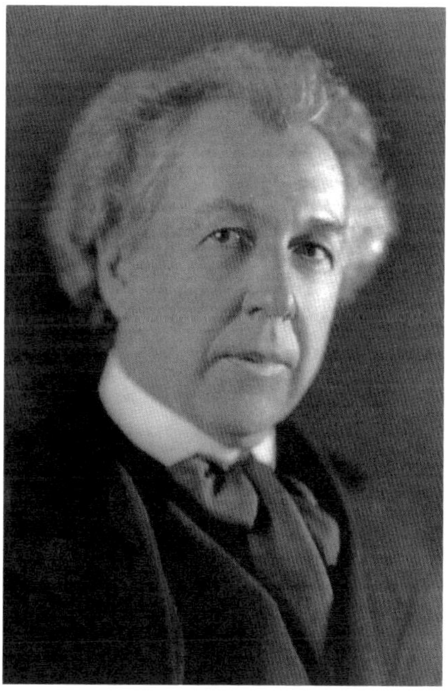

Photograph of architect Frank Lloyd Wright (circa 1926). *Library of Congress (LOC) Prints and Photographs.*

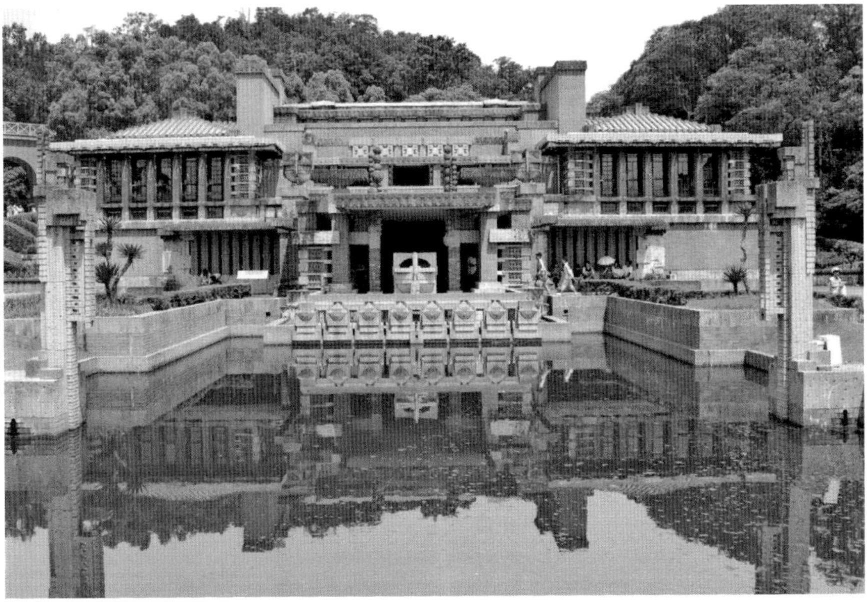

Reconstruction of the main lobby of Wright's Imperial Hotel (circa 2015) at Meiji-mura in Inuyama, Japan. *Photograph by Bariston (Wikimedia Commons).*

Wright was in Chicago that day. Eighteen months earlier, he had been in Tokyo, when the city was struck by a previous earthquake (the largest in thirty years at the time). The building was "in convulsions," Wright wrote, yet he offered reassurances that the structure was purposely built to withstand any earthquake of any magnitude.[16]

Now, on the day of the building's premiere, Wright's credibility was at stake. Had the Imperial Hotel survived? Was it still standing? There were erroneous rumors that the structure had collapsed. But communications had been blocked, and for a number of days, Wright "walked the floor, inconsolable," awaiting a factual update.[17]

In time, confirmation came that the Imperial Hotel was among the few buildings still standing. Not only had it survived the earthquake, but it had even been used as a refuge for displaced victims. Still, news reports continued to claim that it had been substantially damaged. The truth was somewhere in between.

Ties to Mason City

In an effort to quell the rumors, Wright reached out to a California-based public relations expert named Merle Armitage, who was also an acquaintance. Armitage was "an old friend" of the architect's son, Frank Lloyd Wright Jr. (known professionally as Lloyd Wright), who was working at the time as a Hollywood film set designer and residential architect.[18]

Armitage was a book designer and arts impresario, the manager of the Los Angeles Philharmonic Auditorium and would also later become the art director of *Look* magazine. His promotional efforts on Wright's behalf were presumably effective, and today it is widely conceded that Wright's Imperial Hotel (although damaged) was largely resistant to earthquakes.

Whenever this curious story is told, it is rarely mentioned that Wright and Armitage had something else in common: both men had important ties to a small city in north-central Iowa. It was the county seat of Cerro Gordo County called Mason City.

Mason City was, in fact, Merle Armitage's birthplace. Born in 1893 on a farm southeast of the city, he had grown up in that community, then resettled with his parents when his father (one of the earliest livestock farmers to raise corn-fed beef cattle) moved his business interests to Lawrence, Kansas, and after that to Texas.

The Armitage family was no longer living in Mason City when, in 1908, in the course of several visits to the town, Frank Lloyd Wright was commissioned by two local attorneys, James E.E. Markley and James E. Blythe (both on the board of directors of a major city bank), to design a multipurpose building that would include a bank, an adjoining hotel, their own law offices and rentable retail spaces as well. Located beside a downtown park, the hotel was named the Park Inn, while the bank was officially known as the City National Bank.[19]

Stockman House

On an early visit to Mason City, Wright was introduced to Dr. George and Eleanor (Chaffin) Stockman, a local physician and his wife who were Markley's friends and neighbors.

Eleanor Stockman was an impassioned advocate of the National American Woman Suffrage Association. Her sister, Fannie Chaffin, was a longtime

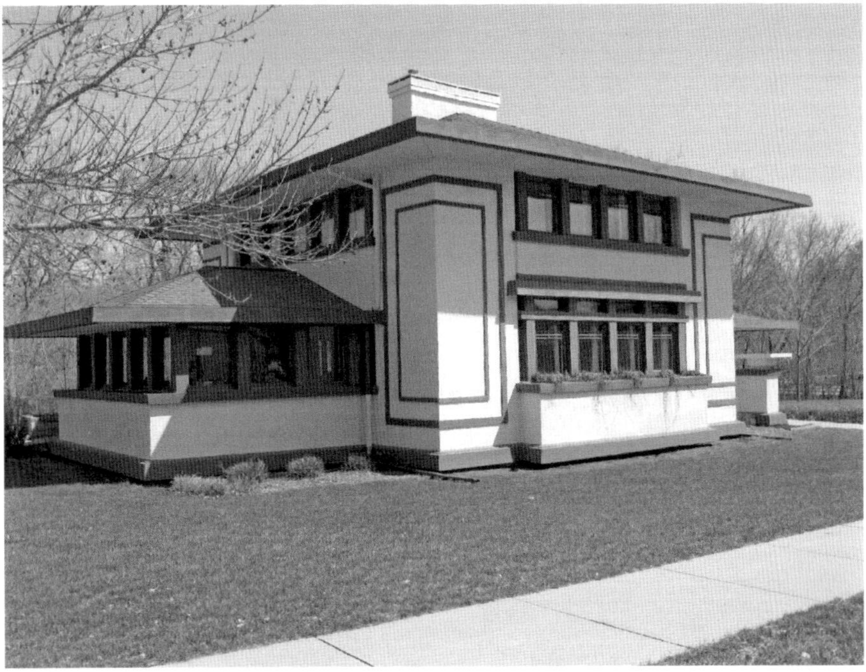

Two views of the George C. Stockman House in Mason City, Iowa, in 2007. *Photographs by Pamela V. White (Wikimedia Commons).*

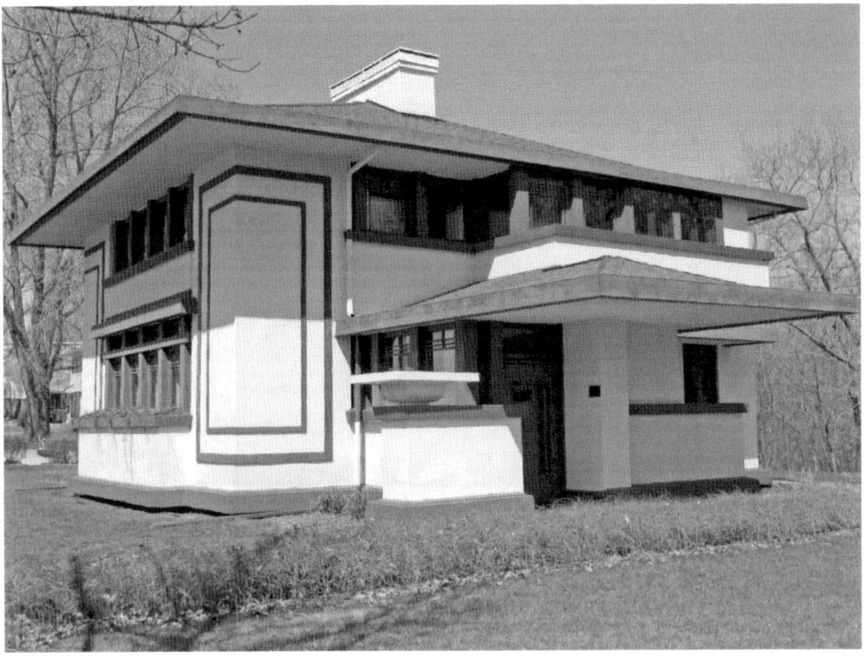

secretary to that organization's president, Carrie Chapman Catt. The latter had grown up in nearby Charles City, Iowa, and had also recently served as a teacher and the first superintendent of schools in Mason City.[20]

The Stockmans approached Wright about designing a two-story, four-bedroom home, both compact and affordable. In response, Wright proposed that he rework an existing plan that he had already published in the *Ladies' Home Journal* called "A Fireproof House for $5,000."[21]

Prior to that, as early as 1903, one of Wright's associates, Walter Burley Griffin (while employed in Wright's studio), had used a similar building plan for the Robert Lamp House in Madison, Wisconsin. A shared characteristic of these and other comparable homes is their "open floor plan" in which there are no dividing walls between the living room and dining room. As a result, these critical zones of activity blend into an L-shape, with a family hearth in the center.[22]

The Stockman House (as it is now commonly known) was completed in 1908. By 1924, Dr. Stockman had retired, and both he and his wife were failing in health. After Eleanor Stockman died that year, the house was sold. In subsequent years, it passed from owner to owner until 1987. Increasingly in disrepair and threatened with demolition (to make way for a church parking lot), it was heroically rescued by a civic-minded community group, which in 1989 moved it to a setting four blocks down the street, raised funds to restore it and opened it as a museum in 1992. By that remarkable effort, a modest yet pivotal landmark was saved for future generations.[23]

Through continued efforts by the River City Society for Historic Preservation, adjacent property was acquired just north of the Stockman House, and in 2011, the Robert E. McCoy Architectural Interpretive Center was completed. Designed by Iowa architect Robert Broshar in a manner that pays homage to both Frank Lloyd Wright and Walter Burley Griffin, it functions year-round as a museum and gift shop facility that offers instructional lectures, collectibles and self-guided tours of all architectural highlights in Mason City.[24]

SUCCESS AND SCANDAL

In planning the City National Bank and Park Inn, Wright made use of what he had learned from previous building projects. Likewise, while working on these Mason City commissions, he gained in ways that strengthened

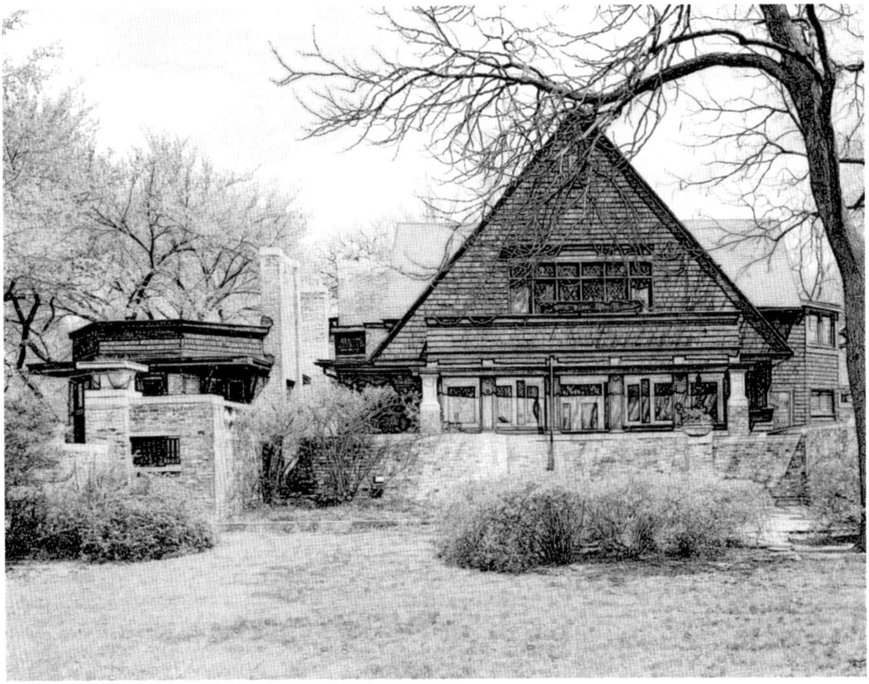

Frank Lloyd Wright's home and studio in Oak Park, Illinois. *Historic American Buildings Survey, LOC Prints and Photographs.*

his subsequent efforts, notably the Midway Gardens (in Chicago) and the Imperial Hotel (in Tokyo). Wright's Mason City projects (the Stockman House and the City National Bank and Park Inn) were completed between 1908 and 1910.

His Mason City clients were delighted with Wright's accomplishments, and there were rumors of future commissions. But before any of those could be realized, he was publicly disgraced by an outrageous personal scandal, in the course of which he abandoned his wife and six children and went to Europe for a year with the wife of one of his clients.[25]

As it turned out, Wright had been in love for several years with an Oak Park neighbor named Martha ("Mamah") Borthwick Cheney (pronounced "MAY-mah CHEE-ny"). Originally from Boone, Iowa, she herself was the mother of two young children.[26]

It was largely because of this scandal (gossip-laced reports of which were front-page stories in the news) that, as Katherine Rodeghier recently wrote in the *Chicago Tribune*, Wright "wasn't exactly run out of town [Mason City]; he was asked never to return."[27] While some uncertainty remains, it is usually assumed that Wright never again set foot in Mason City. While he undoubtedly had access to photographs of the finished buildings, it may be that he never saw the City National Bank and Park Inn in their completed physical state.

In October 1909, Wright and Mamah Borthwick Cheney hurriedly left for Europe.[28] During their year-long absence, the actual construction of the Mason City bank and inn was managed by a Wright associate, Chicago architect William Drummond, who in addition agreed to take on the design of another Mason City residence: the Curtis Yelland House at 7 River Heights Drive.[29]

Following Wright's return from Europe in October 1910, he was commissioned to design the Midway Gardens, an elaborate concert garden and restaurant on Chicago's South Side.[30]

Most likely, Wright and Merle Armitage first became acquainted in 1915. The latter was in Chicago that year, working as a manager and publicity agent for stage and concert performers. The great Russian ballerina Anna Pavlova was featured at the Midway Gardens several times that summer, in addition to other now legendary performers, including the Ballet Russes (Russian Ballet), operatic tenor Enrico Caruso and others.[31]

It was during this time that Wright's career as an architect was substantially reestablished when he was commissioned to design the Imperial Hotel in Tokyo.

WRIGHT AND KINDERGARTEN

When and how did Frank Lloyd Wright, an up-and-coming architect from the burgeoning Windy City, become linked historically to a city as small and seemingly out of the way as Mason City, Iowa? One answer—believe it or not—is *kindergarten*.

Kindergarten in this case does not refer to preschool as we know it now but to the original kindergarten (or "children's garden") of German educator Friedrich Froebel that began in Europe in the 1830s. Froebel's kindergarten was not a literal garden (although, at times, its pupils did raise plants) but rather a radical new approach to early childhood teaching.[32]

Froebel challenged the customary practice of treating children as if they were adults in miniature, to be molded by rigid restrictions. To Froebel, children were first and foremost pliable minds. Having studied crystallography and forestry, he compared young children to immature plants.

Froebel believed that children, like seedlings, should be gently and patiently cared for. With tolerance and understanding, they should be helped to gradually learn and grow through participatory ("hands-on") activities, such as singing, dancing and gardening—and by self-directed play.

It was Froebel's idea, as once described by Arts and Crafts advocate Elbert Hubbard,

> *that the child was a human flower, and the school should be a garden where souls could blossom in the sunshine of love. …He* [Froebel] *utilized the tendency to play; just as we in degree use the tides of the sea and the winds that blow to turn the wheels of trade.*[33]

Hubbard, the now famous founder of the Roycroft artists' community in East Aurora, New York, had known Frank Lloyd Wright in Chicago. He had also been a vice-president of the Larkin Company, a pioneering and hugely successful mail-order firm in Buffalo, New York, for which Wright designed,

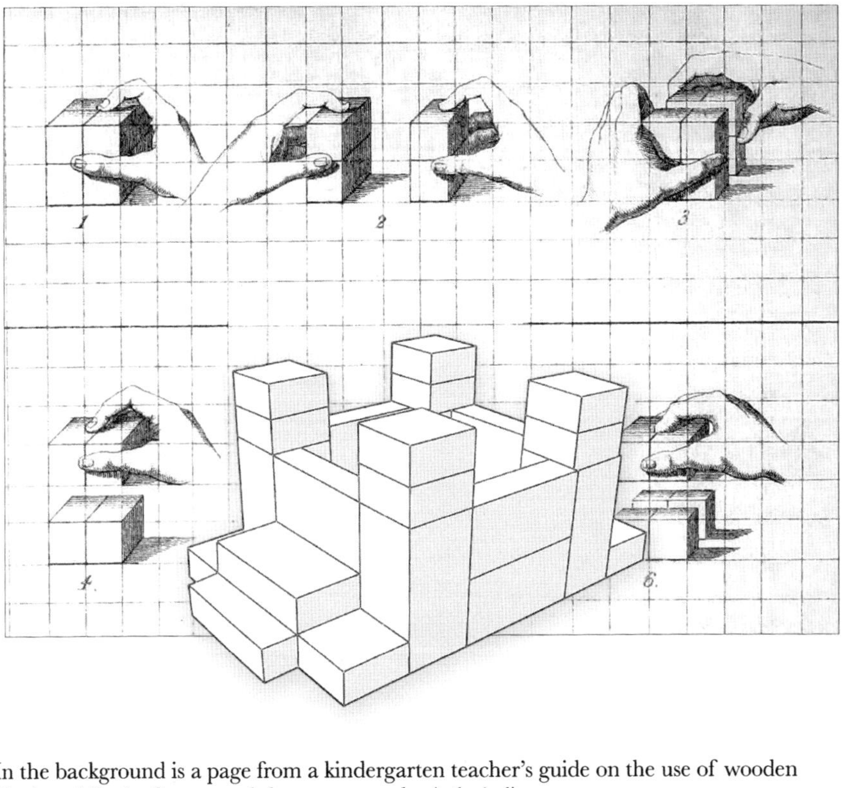

In the background is a page from a kindergarten teacher's guide on the use of wooden blocks, while the foreground shows one result. *Author's diagram.*

in 1904, the acclaimed Larkin Building, the company's administrative offices. Soon after, Wright also designed private homes for several Larkin executives, two of whom were married to Hubbard's sisters, including John D. Larkin, the company's chief executive officer.[34]

Having been influenced by the aesthetic movement, Hubbard and Wright (and Griffin) dressed "like artists," wearing longish page-boy hairstyles and conspicuous Buster Brown cravats.[35]

To facilitate hands-on learning, Froebel devised a series of educational toys called "gifts." Over time, each of his pupils was given the same set of these components (about twenty), one at a time, in a deliberate sequence.[36]

The most familiar of these were his famous sets of wooden blocks (smooth, unpainted maple blocks with no carved letters or other designs), which each child could put together in various ways to produce the widest variety of combinations.

Froebel had begun his own kindergarten in Germany in the late 1830s, but it quickly spread across Europe and to other continents. In 1856, the first American kindergarten (German speaking) was started in Watertown, Wisconsin, less than ten miles from Ixonia, where Wright's ancestors settled. Less than twenty years later, there were 556 kindergartens in the United States.[37]

Origin and Beliefs

Frank Lloyd Wright was born Frank Lincoln Wright in Wisconsin in 1867 (for years, he listed his birth year as 1869, but records indicate otherwise) and grew up near Richland Center, about one hundred miles from Watertown, site of the country's first kindergarten.[38] His mother (née Anna Lloyd Jones) had been trained as a teacher, while his father (William Wright) was a traveling Baptist preacher and musician.

Unfortunately, his father's inability to provide a reliable income (plus other complications, not always the fault of his father) eventually contributed to William Wright's departure from the family (at his wife's suggestion) and the collapse of the couple's marriage. Coincident with the ensuing divorce (filed by his father and not contested), son Frank changed his middle name from Lincoln to Lloyd, as a way to spurn his father and to underscore his loyalty to his mother's family.[39]

In contrast to his father, Wright's mother and her relatives were wealthy, self-assured and well established. Of Welsh ancestry, they were

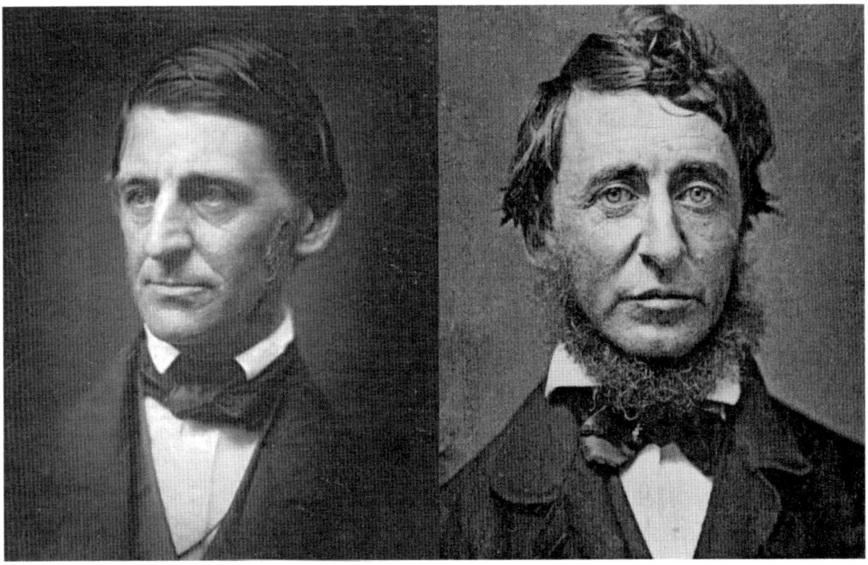

Transcendentalists Ralph Waldo Emerson and Henry David Thoreau. *Wikimedia Commons.*

impassioned free-thinkers who lived by the motto "The truth against the world."[40] They were outspoken adherents of Unitarianism and admirers of the writings of the New England transcendentalists, the most famous of whom were Ralph Waldo Emerson, Henry David Thoreau and Margaret Fuller.

Wright's uncle (his mother's brother) was Jenkin Lloyd Jones ("Uncle Jenk"), founder and longtime patriarch of the All Souls Church in Chicago, a church that welcomed all faiths, Christian or otherwise. He also traveled to midwestern cities, including Mason City, Iowa, to proselytize.

In Mason City, among Uncle Jenk's acquaintances was Mary Emsley, James E.E. Markley's mother-in-law, a staunch Unitarian and ardent suffragist who sometimes traveled to Richland Center, Wisconsin, to attend Jones's Chautauqua presentations.[41]

Wright's mother had two unmarried sisters, Ellen (Nell) and Jane Lloyd Jones, who were also teachers. In 1887, they founded a progressive coeducational school on the Lloyd Jones family estate, about twenty-five miles from Richland Center, near Spring Green.

The six-hundred-acre family estate was in Jones Valley, which local people sarcastically called "the valley of the God-Almighty Joneses."[42] The property had been acquired by Wright's maternal grandfather in the mid-nineteenth century.

Wright's aunts' school, called Hillside Home School, was initially housed in a wood-frame, Shingle-style building designed by their architect nephew at age nineteen. Years later, he designed an alternative building of stone. The construction of that second building was supervised by Wright associate Walter Burley Griffin (who would later play a central role in Mason City architecture). It officially opened in 1902.

That same year, one of the daughters of Mason City's James E.E. and Lilly (Emsley) Markley (who would advocate commissioning Wright to design the City National Bank and Park Inn) enrolled as a student there. Soon after, a second daughter enrolled as well.[43]

Froebel at the World's Fair

A quarter of a century earlier, in 1876, Frank Lloyd Wright's mother had attended the Centennial Exposition in Philadelphia, a one-hundred-year celebration of the origins of the United States.[44]

While there, she saw an exhibition about the kindergarten movement and soon after bought a set of Froebel blocks (which by then were being sold by game manufacturer Milton Bradley). She shared these

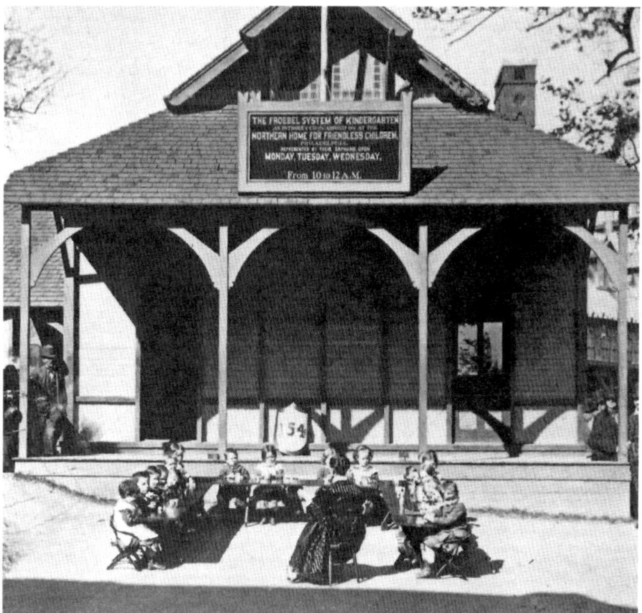

Visitors to the 1876 Centennial Exposition in Philadelphia were able to observe a kindergarten class. *LOC Prints and Photographs.*

with her son and two daughters, but especially with Frank, whom she had predicted (even before he was actually born) would grow up to be an architect.

Of course, Wright's mother had no way of knowing just how true her prediction would be. In 1991, more than thirty years after Wright's death, he would be officially honored as "the greatest American architect of all time" by the American Institute of Architects—an organization that, during his lifetime, he had frequently poked fun at and refused to be a member of. Much earlier than that, on January 17, 1938, he had also been featured on the cover of *Time* magazine.

In his writings, Wright repeatedly remembered how his mother had introduced him to Froebel's geometric blocks, long after kindergarten age, most likely when he was nine or ten: "For several years I sat at the little kindergarten table top…and played…[with] these smooth wooden maple blocks. …[They] are in my fingers to this day."[45]

As documented by Norman Brosterman, Wright was one of a number of European and American artists, designers and architects (and those in other professions as well) from the same time period who, as children, were introduced to Froebel's blocks and comparable construction toys.[46] In Wright's case, the influence was doubly strong because, later, as a parent, he introduced his own children to Froebel's gifts.

In one of the gifts, known as "peas-work," children were provided with a supply of dried peas (or small cork cubes or balls of wax) and toothpicks, with which they could assemble forms.[47] Most likely, the Tinkertoy Construction Set, even if indirectly, was influenced by Froebel's peas-work gift, although its immediate model is said to have been sticks and empty spools of thread.

Wright had fond memories of his encounters with hands-on toys like peas-work. But even more greatly influenced by these was architect-engineer R. Buckminster Fuller (interestingly, he was the grandnephew of New England transcendentalist Margaret Fuller).

Born cross-eyed and abnormally farsighted, Fuller (in his own words) "could only see large patterns, houses, trees and outlines of people. …I could see two dark areas on human faces, but I could not see a human eye or a teardrop or a human hair."[48]

Opposite: In kindergarten, Buckminster Fuller made peas and toothpick constructions (top), then later used the same method in his geodesic dome (bottom). *Author's diagram and U.S. Patent 3,203,144, U.S. Patent Office.*

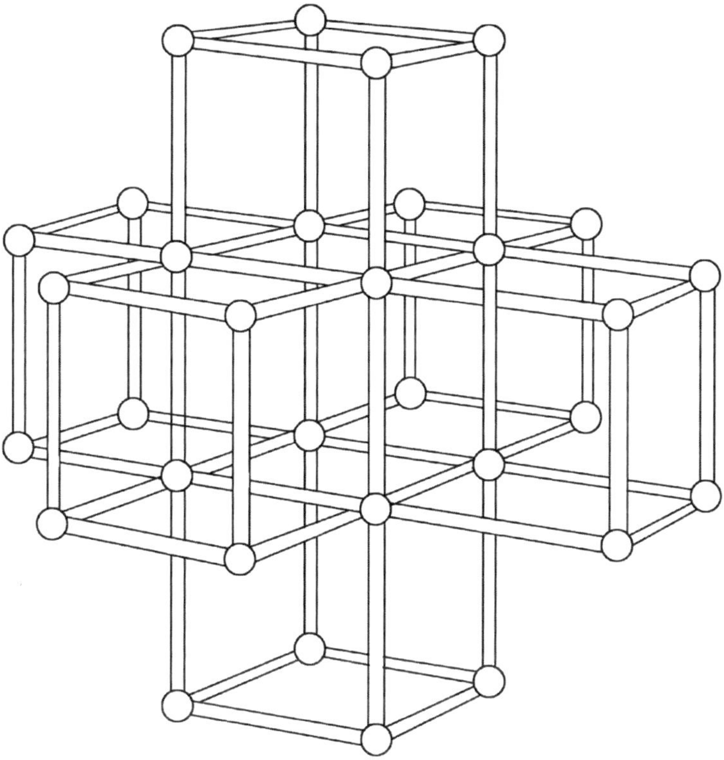

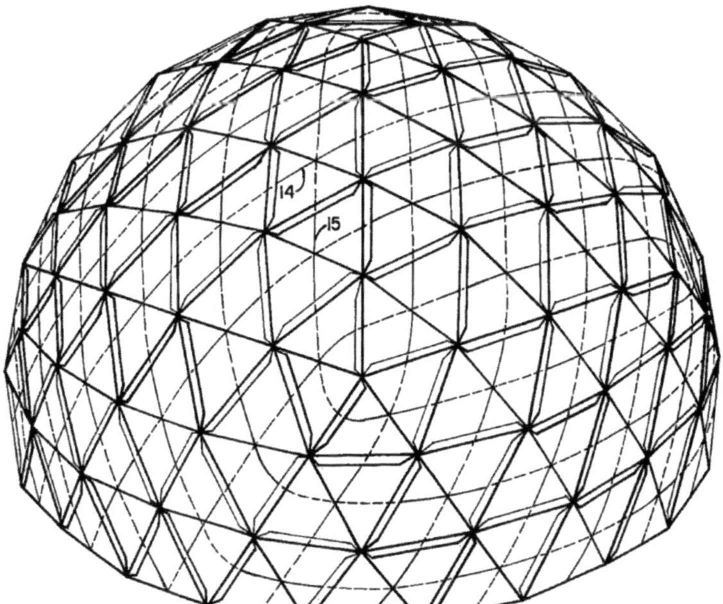
14
15

When Fuller's kindergarten group was given peas and toothpicks, the majority of his classmates made rectangles and cubes, the first solutions that sprang to mind.

Given his visual impairment, Fuller chose instead to make a triangular unit (the "octet truss"), which is structurally stronger and which he would later use as the module for his famous geodesic dome. That same year, he was also fitted with powerful Coke bottle glasses, but even after that, he recalled, "my childhood's spontaneous dependence only upon big patterns has persisted."[49]

Throughout his life, whenever Frank Lloyd Wright was asked what experiences had contributed to his development as an architect, he invariably responded that his two greatest influences had been Froebel's kindergarten blocks and Japanese Ukiyo-e woodcut prints (of which he was a collector and dealer). It is now commonly claimed that these two factors were part of what enabled Wright to see architectural shapes as generic abstract forms, which he called "constructive patterns."[50]

Throughout his career, unlike most people, Wright saw buildings as generalized patterns, as "big picture" whole effects, not as incidental parts. In his own words, he saw a building as "one great thing instead of a quarreling collection of so many little things."[51]

Like Buckminster Fuller, Wright had learned to see holistically—to see layouts or gestalts, as do graphic designers. Their way of seeing was somewhat like looking through the wrong end of a telescope. It was a generalized, overall view—or, as the age-old maxim says, they saw the forest instead of the trees.

Recalling Wright's achievements, as well as those of Fuller and others, a poignant passage comes to mind from William James's *Principles of Psychology*, in which he said that "some people are far more sensitive to resemblances, and far more ready to point out wherein they consist, than others are. They are the wits, the poets, the inventors, the scientific men, the practical geniuses."[52]

Primacy of Unity

In his autobiography, kindergarten founder Friedrich Froebel stated that "all is unity, all rests in unity, all springs from unity, strives for and leads up to unity, and returns to unity at last."[53]

Early in his teaching career, Froebel had devised the second gift in his series, consisting of a wooden ball and a cube, with a cylinder in between.

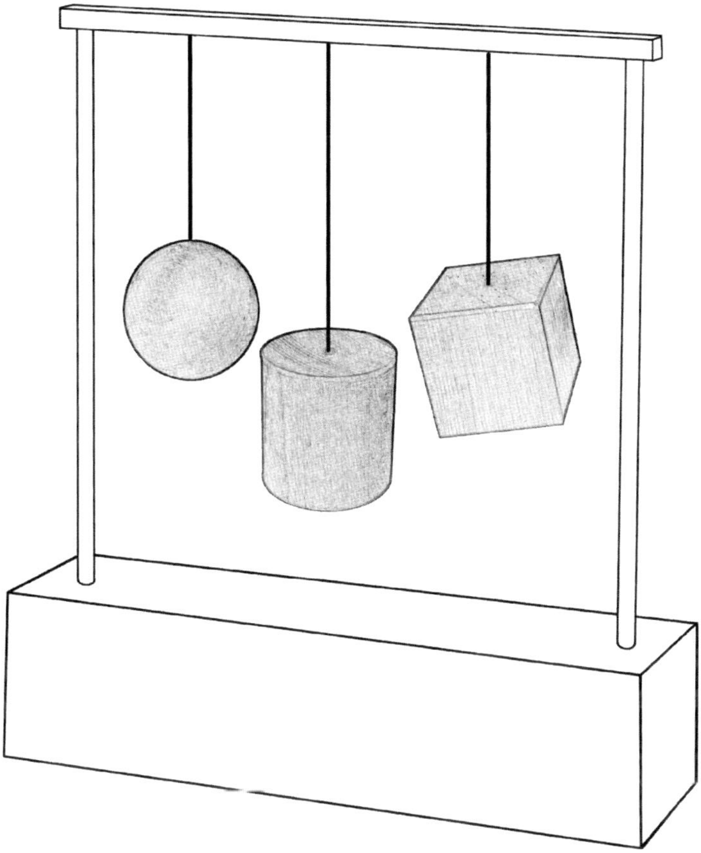

The second kindergarten gift was Friedrich Froebel's favorite, consisting of a wooden sphere, a cylinder and a cube. *Author's drawing.*

This was his favorite of all the gifts, since none of the others so powerfully showed the unity of opposites.

A ball and a cube are typically assumed to be radically different shape types, yet Froebel in the second gift showed that both those fundamental shapes are found within the cylinder. The cylinder looks circular when viewed from the end but looks square like a cube when observed from the side. Further, when suspended from a string or transformed into spinning tops, these shapes look even more alike.

Regarding this second gift, Brosterman has said:

> *Without mirrors, nothing up his sleeve, and right before their eyes, Froebel, in a sleight-of-hand worthy of a resourceful magician, created the ultimate*

gambit—a straightforward demonstration of cosmic mutuality and universal connectedness that even a child could understand.[54]

If Wright's way of looking is indebted to Froebel, he was just as strongly influenced by Unitarianism and transcendentalism, which were related but differing trends at the close of the nineteenth century.

All three phenomena (kindergarten, Unitarianism and transcendentalism) had attributes that confirmed their connectedness, the most important of which was unity. It is not surprising, then, that the person who founded the first English-language kindergarten in the United States, Elizabeth Palmer Peabody, was a leading transcendentalist and an associate of Margaret Fuller.

In Wright's autobiography, when he described the Unitarianism of his Lloyd Jones relatives (whose meeting places bore such names as Unity Temple, Unity Church and Unity Chapel), he said, "Unity was their watchword, the sign and symbol that thrilled them, the unity of all things."[55]

In the transcendentalism of Emerson and Thoreau—as well as in other traditions that emphasize the bond between spirituality and nature—there was no rigid distinction between man and nature.

Thoreau once told a story about a sparrow that "alight[ed] on my shoulder for a moment, while I was hoeing in a village garden, and I felt that I was more distinguished by that circumstance than I should have been by any epaulet I could have worn."[56]

To the transcendentalists, we are one with nature. In Wright's case, he repeatedly expressed the view that nature is a manifestation of God and that "Nature should be spelled with a capital N."[57] Spirituality is attendant at all times and in all places so that a person might worship alone in the woods as suitably as congregate in a designated meeting hall on a particular day of the week.

It may seem ironic that Wright designed a number of churches (including synagogues) during his life for a variety of religious groups, not just Unitarians. In 1957, in an interview with television journalist Mike Wallace, when asked if he attended church, Wright replied, "I attend the greatest of all churches"—by which, of course, he meant Nature.[58]

As a result, he continued, he was free "to build churches for other people," in the sense that "if I belonged to any one church, they couldn't ask me to build a church for them. But because my church is elemental, fundamental, I can build [a place of worship] for anybody."[59]

EUROPEAN INTERLUDE

When Frank Lloyd Wright and Mamah Borthwick Cheney left hurriedly for Europe in October 1909, it was not just to escape the lurid accounts of their personal lives in American newspapers.

There were other reasons as well, foremost of which was an opportunity for Wright to travel to Berlin (he had never visited Europe before) and to collaborate with a prestigious publisher named Ernst Wasmuth in producing a large-format, two-volume folio of his finest architectural work, spanning from 1893 through 1909.[60]

The first volume of this publication began with an introduction by Wright, essentially amounting to a manifesto for what would in time become well known as Prairie School architecture.

When initially published, the German title of that first volume was *Ausgeführte Bauten und Entwürfe von Frank Lloyd Wright* (*Drawings and Plans of Frank Lloyd Wright*), but it soon became widely referred to as the *Wasmuth Portfolio*.[61]

Featured in the *Wasmuth Portfolio* were numerous line-work lithographs of his architectural projects, with floor plans and perspective views. Among the projects that were prominently featured were Wright's three buildings in Mason City: the Stockman House and the City National Bank and Park Inn.

Of the book's illustrations, about half were rendered by Marion Mahony, one of the most talented associates in Wright's Oak Park architectural firm. These drawings were purposely similar to Japanese Ukiyo-e woodcuts. As Wright himself admitted, their indebtedness "to Japanese ideals, these renderings themselves sufficiently acknowledge."[62]

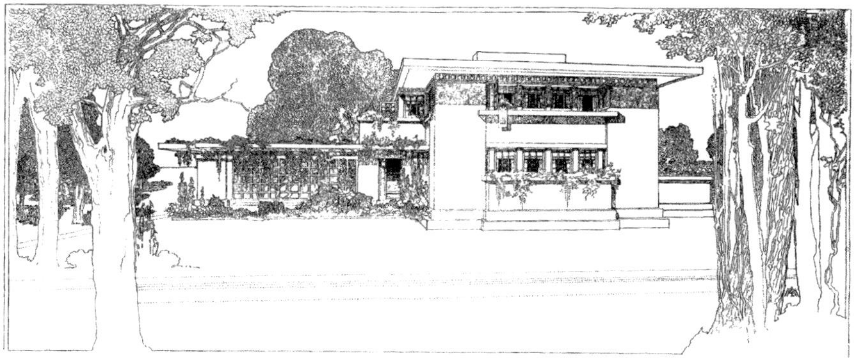

Wright's design for "A Fireproof Home for $5,000," the plans for which were used for the Stockman House, among others. Wasmuth Portfolio *(1910)*.

Mahony was among the first women to study architecture at MIT and one of the first to become a licensed American architect. Hired by Wright in 1895, for fifteen years she was a vital contributor (albeit in the background) to his architectural triumphs and later even more so to the subsequent achievements of Walter Burley Griffin, who began to work for Wright in 1901 and whom she married in 1911.

In fact, it was Walter Burley Griffin and Marion Mahony Griffin, more than Wright, who solidified the legacy of Mason City (and Rock Crest/Rock Glen specifically) as an architectural landmark—one that scholar Paul Kruty described as "a timeless masterpiece melding landscape, planning, and architecture."[63]

The importance of the *Wasmuth Portfolio* to Frank Lloyd Wright's career cannot be overstated. When he left for Europe, he was already in his forties. While his work had not been ignored in America (it had been featured in various periodicals, as well as in a monograph), it was at best insufficiently praised, and by 1909, debates about his architecture were outpaced by the gossip regarding his life.

The *Wasmuth Portfolio* was the first international showcase of Wright's architecture, and it served as a two-pronged occasion: It called attention to his work among American architects when they saw it regarded so seriously by a prestigious audience from abroad.[64] At the same time, it introduced his achievements to a generation of young European architects, who immediately sensed the connections between Wright and their own explorations.

Among young architects at the time, the most sought-after place of training and employment in Germany was the studio of architect and designer Peter Behrens, who had recently taken on the role of the first corporate designer in history.

In 1907, Behrens had been retained as "artistic advisor" (design director) for the company AEG (Allgemeine Elektrizitäts-Gesellschaft, or German General Electric).

In that capacity, Behrens' studio was responsible for developing the "brand" of the company, the "style" of what it stood for—its corporate logo, its products, its packaging and its advertising.

He was also its chief architect, most notably in 1910, when he designed the famous AEG Turbine Factory.[65]

Arts and Crafts Movement

Initially trained as an artist, Behrens had gradually turned to architecture, interwoven with art and design. In so doing, he was only one of many artists turned designers whose careers had been inspired by the example of British designer William Morris.

Morris was the revered patriarch of the Arts and Crafts movement, so named because it tried to soften the arrogant class distinctions between glorified "artists" and denigrated "craftsmen," the lowly designers of functional things.

Morris' efforts had begun in the late 1850s, when he took on the responsibility of furnishing his own new home, called Red House (designed for Morris and his bride by his architect friend Philip Webb). Soon after, he established Morris and Company, a design firm that produced a wide range of interior accessories, such as wall tapestries, textiles, wallpaper, art glass windows and furniture.[66]

In 1895, inspired by Morris' example, a Belgian-born artist turned architect/designer named Henry van de Velde designed his own home (called Bloemenwerf) outside Brussels and produced its interior furnishings, too.[67] Four years later, this idea was taken further by none other than Peter Behrens, who designed his home (called Behrens Haus), as well as its furnishings and accessories.

It is important to realize that Behrens' house was one of seven experimental residences in a planned community setting in Darmstadt, Germany, known as the Darmstadt Artists' Colony. Located on a hill above the city (called Mathildenhöhe), the neighborhood opened officially in 1901.[68]

This cluster of Darmstadt artists' homes is of particular relevance here because, in ways, it was a precedent for what would take place in Mason City a decade later.

It was at that time, after the completion of the City National Bank and Park Inn Hotel (by which point Wright had been dismissed), that Wright's former associate Walter Burley Griffin was commissioned to design an architectural neighborhood in Mason City (to be known as Rock Crest/Rock Glen), within which were constructed a group of gem-like Prairie School homes.

It is of additional interest because, while Wright was visiting Germany, he made a targeted effort to visit the Darmstadt Artists' Colony, where most of the homes (with the exception of Behrens' house) had been designed by Josef Maria Olbrich, an Austrian architect who had co-founded the Vienna Secession and designed the famous Secession Building in Vienna.[69]

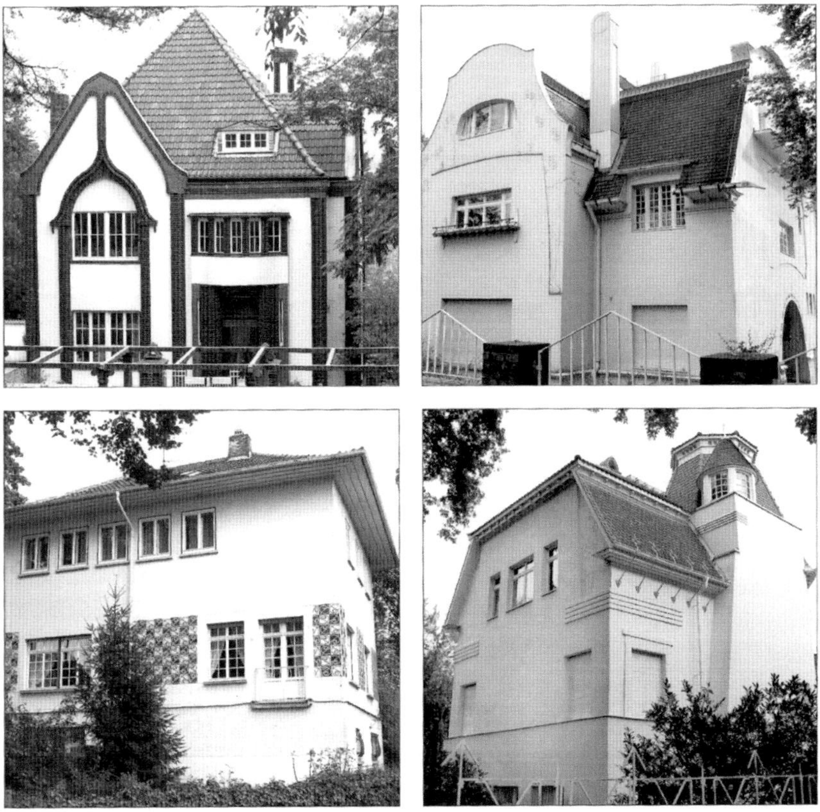

Houses in the Darmstadt Artists' Colony (circa 1901). At top left is Peter Behrens' house. The remaining three were designed by Josef Maria Olbrich. *Photographs by Storflix (Wikimedia Commons).*

Wright was acquainted with Olbrich's designs, some of which had won prestigious prizes at the 1904 Exposition in St. Louis. Wright went to St. Louis to tour the exhibits there, which included works by Olbrich, Peter Behrens, Josef Hoffmann and other Europeans.[70] When he returned to Chicago from St. Louis, he was so excited that he paid the travel expenses of one of his studio associates, Barry Byrne, to attend the exhibition himself.

Later, Byrne himself would play a role in the development of Mason City's Rock Crest/Rock Glen community. In 1908, he worked briefly in the Griffin's studio and then established his own practice in California.

In 1914, when Griffin and his wife, Marion Mahony, moved to Australia (permanently as it turned out) to design that country's new capital of Canberra, Byrne was contracted to manage Griffin's architectural firm.

As a result, he guided the completion of the Rock Crest/Rock Glen neighborhood, where he is also credited with overseeing Griffin's design (if not always as Griffin had planned) of several Prairie School houses, along with two designed by him.[71]

After arriving in Germany, Wright was eager to travel to Darmstadt to see its artist colony residences. While there, he had also hoped to meet Olbrich, not realizing that the forty-year-old architect had died of leukemia a few months earlier.[72] It is often suggested that there are strong correlations between some of Olbrich's earlier work (his Vienna Secession Building for one) and Wright's Unity Temple and the Larkin Building. Did Olbrich influence Wright? Or did Wright influence the Europeans? No one knows for certain, and most likely we will never know. For whatever reason, Wright was surprised (and apparently not displeased) when he was introduced to German architects in Berlin as the "American Olbrich."[73]

Today, Mason City is a treasure-trove of architectural delights. But it would not be quite so amazing if it could claim only to be the home of three Frank Lloyd Wright buildings.

Of equal significance is the Rock Crest/Rock Glen neighborhood, which is of greater distinction than is usually realized. That unique neighborhood, as architect Jonathan Lipman said, is "the major focus of Prairie architecture outside of Chicago…the largest collection of Prairie School houses unified by a common natural setting in the world."[74]

When Griffin's planned neighborhood is combined with Wright's three buildings, it may not be undue to say that Mason City is an architectural heart of the prairie—a Darmstadt of the Middle West.

Gesamtkunstwerk

In Europe, among architects and designers in the late nineteenth century, the practice of designing a building as a coherently unified whole acquired the name of *Gesamtkunstwerk*.[75]

The term was used initially—outside of architecture—in 1847 and was soon after popularized by the German composer Richard Wagner, who used it as a tag line for elaborate performances ("opera and drama") in which all the arts (dance, theater, music, literature and the visual arts) were combined in one production. Dissembling its German components—*Gesamt* means "total," *kunst* means "art" and *werk* is "work"—the translation to English is "total work of art."

Late in the nineteenth century, when the term was widely adopted among architects, it signified that it was no longer acceptable to merely plan a building's shell (walls, rooms, doors and windows) and then sign off and be done with the project. Instead, a building should be a unified composition in which all its subsets are compatible with the total effect—beginning with the building site, its shell, its interior furnishings and other accessories.

Frank Lloyd Wright apparently spoke little, if any, German. In his writings, it is doubtful if he ever used the German word Gesamtkunstwerk, but in the *Wasmuth Portfolio* introduction, he talks about a dwelling as "a complete work of art."[76]

An equivalent phrase that he frequently used was "organic form." By that, he meant that all aspects of a building should have the same functional duality as parts of the body, words in a sentence or members of society.[77]

Each part should function as a whole, a discrete fragment, while at the same time contributing to a larger unit, a unified totality. While each part has its particular task (the thumb, for example, does certain things well, others not), it must also work for the good of the whole. The same can be said of ingredients that compose a house, a bank, a hotel or other structure.

"Organic," according to Wright associate Barry Byrne, "was his favorite word. When you look at a tree, it is a magnificent example of an organic whole. All parts belong together, not by labels or intellectual means, they just belong, as fingers belong to one's hands."[78]

In the *Wasmuth Portfolio*, Wright said of organic architecture that "it is quite impossible to consider the building as one thing, its furnishings another and its setting and environment still another. The spirit, in which these buildings are conceived, sees all these together at work as one thing."[79]

In reading this and other passages, while knowing that other European architects and designers (among them Henry van de Velde, Peter Behrens, Josef Maria Olbrich, Charles Rennie Mackintosh, Josef Hoffmann, Gerrit Rietveld) were enchanted by the concept of Gesamtkunstwerk, one can imagine the fervor with which they and other architects read Wright's inspiring essay on organic form and carefully studied his buildings as well.[80]

In Berlin, in the year Wright's folio first appeared, there were twenty to thirty employees in Peter Behrens' studio. Among his apprentices were people who would soon become some of the most famous architects of the twentieth century, among them Le Corbusier, Mies van der Rohe and

Walter Gropius (who would later be founder-director of the Bauhaus, the most influential art and design school in modern history).

It is sometimes claimed (true or not) that in Behrens' Berlin studio, when the *Wasmuth Portfolio* was released, the activities of the company were halted for the day so that the studio's young architects could have sufficient time to study Wright's publication.

Organic Form

In Europe, the public reaction to the practice of Gesamtkunstwerk was no less controversial than was Frank Lloyd Wright's insistence on organic form. At one time or another, architects on both sides of the Atlantic were accused of taking it to extremes and of behaving despotically toward their clients.

Among those satirized was Belgian-born architect and designer Henry van de Velde, who designed not only his family's home and all its furnishings but also matching outfits for his wife and children (intended to be worn at home).[81]

A famous apocryphal story reports that van de Velde once reproached a client who, although he was wearing the slippers designed by van de Velde to be worn in that house, was scolded for wearing them in the wrong room.

"They were designed to be worn in the bedroom!" he admonished his dumbfounded client.[82]

During these same years, Viennese artist/designer Gustav Klimt collaborated with his companion, Emilie Flöge, on the design of upscale, exquisitely designed "art dresses."[83]

Likewise, Frank Lloyd Wright is said to have made architecturally appropriate outfits for his wife Catherine (of which photographs still exist), as well as for his clients' wives in the Coonley, Robie and Dana homes.[84]

In the United States, Wright's reputation (deserved or not) has often been one of intimidating his clients. Given his commitment to organic form, he probably would have preferred to have been even more inflexible in insisting on what was permissible in an idealized Wrightian setting.

This was a continuing problem because his clients too often assumed (after all, it was *their* home, which *they* had financed most likely at a greater cost than the architect had initially estimated) that they could fill up their new masterpiece with the tasteless stuff they already owned.

At one point, he suggested that "about four-fifths of the contents of nearly every home could be given away with good effect to that home. But the

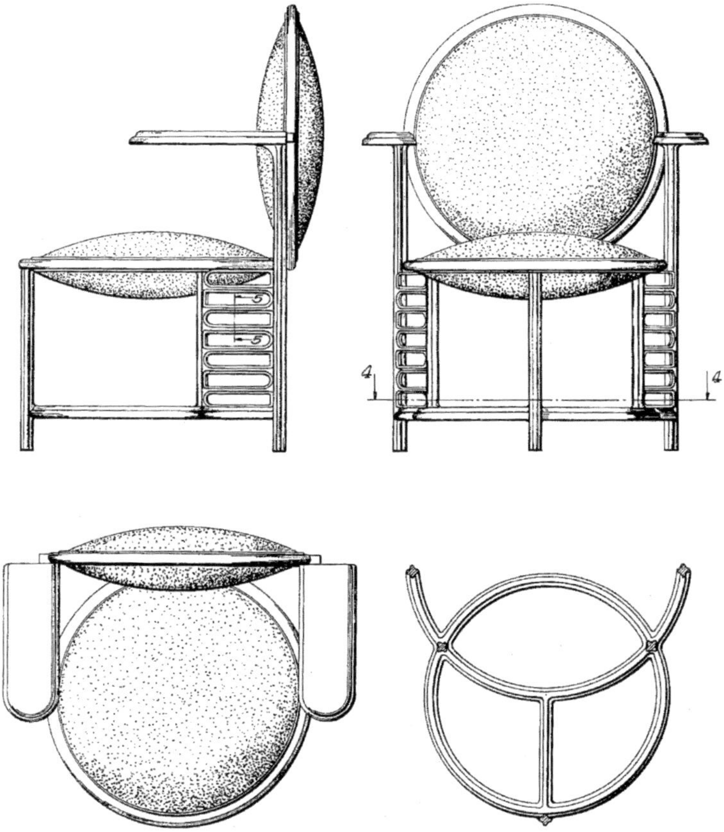

Patent drawings for Wright's office chair for the Johnson Wax Office Building in Racine, Wisconsin (circa 1939). *U.S. Patent D108,473, U.S. Patent Office.*

things given away might go on to poison some other home. So why not at once destroy undesirable things…make an end of them?"[85]

Wright himself admitted that few of the houses he designed were "anything but painful to me after the clients moved in…[having] dragged [in] the horrors of the old order along after them."[86] From early on, he addressed this issue (as did others of the same era) by developing his own innovative furniture for each newly designed house.

At times, he was superbly successful at furniture design, and at other times, emphatically not. It was a formidable challenge to make an architectural style align with the functional requirements of furniture, with the result, as he conceded: "I have been black and blue in some spot, somewhere, almost all my life from too intimate contacts with my own furniture."[87]

Desolation and Despair

The complete two-volume *Wasmuth Portfolio* was published in 1911, a few months after Wright returned to Chicago. By then, it was apparent that, unless he gave up his relationship with Mamah Borthwick Cheney and returned to his wife and children, he could not continue to live in Oak Park. He and Mamah would have to relocate.

As a solution, he decided he would design and construct a new Prairie School home (to be named Taliesin, which is Welsh for "shining brow") near Spring Green, Wisconsin, in Jones Valley, on land that his mother had given to him.

The construction of Taliesin was promptly begun, and Wright and Mamah Borthwick (now divorced, she had reverted to her maiden name) moved into the living quarters in the winter of 1911. Meanwhile, Wright took on the design of the Midway Gardens in Chicago, in addition to other commissions. In 1913, he and Mamah traveled to Japan in order to purchase Ukiyo-e woodblock prints for art collectors. During the same trip, he also apparently met with Japanese officials to further discuss the design of the new Imperial Hotel in Tokyo.

And then, the most dreadful tragedy struck. On August 15, 1914, Mamah Borthwick was at Taliesin with her two visiting children (ten and eleven years old), while Wright was in Chicago, working with his architect son, John Lloyd Wright, on plans for the Midway Gardens. Other members of the Taliesin work crew at Spring Green were also present on the grounds.[88]

During the lunch hour, Borthwick and her children were savagely attacked and killed by a domestic servant, a "Barbados Negro" (Wright's term, which is important to mention because the ethnicity of the assailant was invariably emphasized in newspaper reports) who was brandishing a shingling axe.

The assailant then set fire to the building, attacking others as they fled. Seven people were slain that day, others wounded, and much of Taliesin was destroyed.

Emotionally devastated—presumably in greater pain than before or ever again in his life—Wright and his son John returned by train to Spring Green to confront the horrifying reality.

To the credit of Wright and Edwin Cheney (Mamah Borthwick's former husband), the two men made the trip together in a shared railway car—the former to bury the woman he loved and the latter to claim the severed remains of his murdered children.[89]

Not surprisingly, some of the newspaper stories about the murders were no less crude or lurid than had been the earlier articles on the couple's romance.

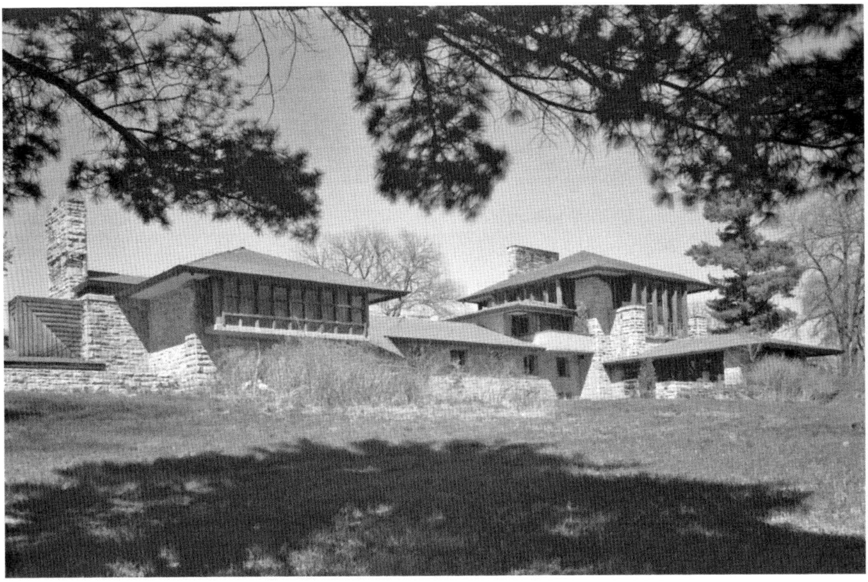

Taliesin East near Spring Green, Wisconsin, after having been rebuilt. *Historic American Buildings Survey, LOC Prints and Photographs.*

Some newspapers even suggested that the slaying of Mamah Borthwick was retribution by the God of the Old Testament for their extramarital lustfulness. In the August 15 issue of the *Detroit Tribune*, an especially insensitive headline read: "Negro Fires 'Love Bungalow.'"

Two days after the attack, an account of the murders appeared on the front page of the *Mason City Globe-Gazette*. It included this sequence of headlines:

> *Wright's Soul Mate Is Slain. Infuriated Negro Cook Kills Three* [sic] *at "Love Bungalow" of Man Well Known in This City. City National Was Designed by Wright. Famous Chicago Architect Who Attracted World-Wide Attention by Love Affairs, Planned Some of the Finest Buildings of Mason City, Including the Dr. Stockman House.*

At the Taliesin crime scene, the fire continued to smolder for days, followed by a freak hailstorm, with more destruction being caused by water damage. In the basement, Wright had been storing the printing plates of the *Wasmuth Portfolio* and finished but unbound copies. In the end, only thirty undamaged copies survived.

Mamah Borthwick was buried quietly in the Lloyd Jones ancestral cemetery at Taliesin. At her grave site, Wright was left by himself in order to shovel dirt

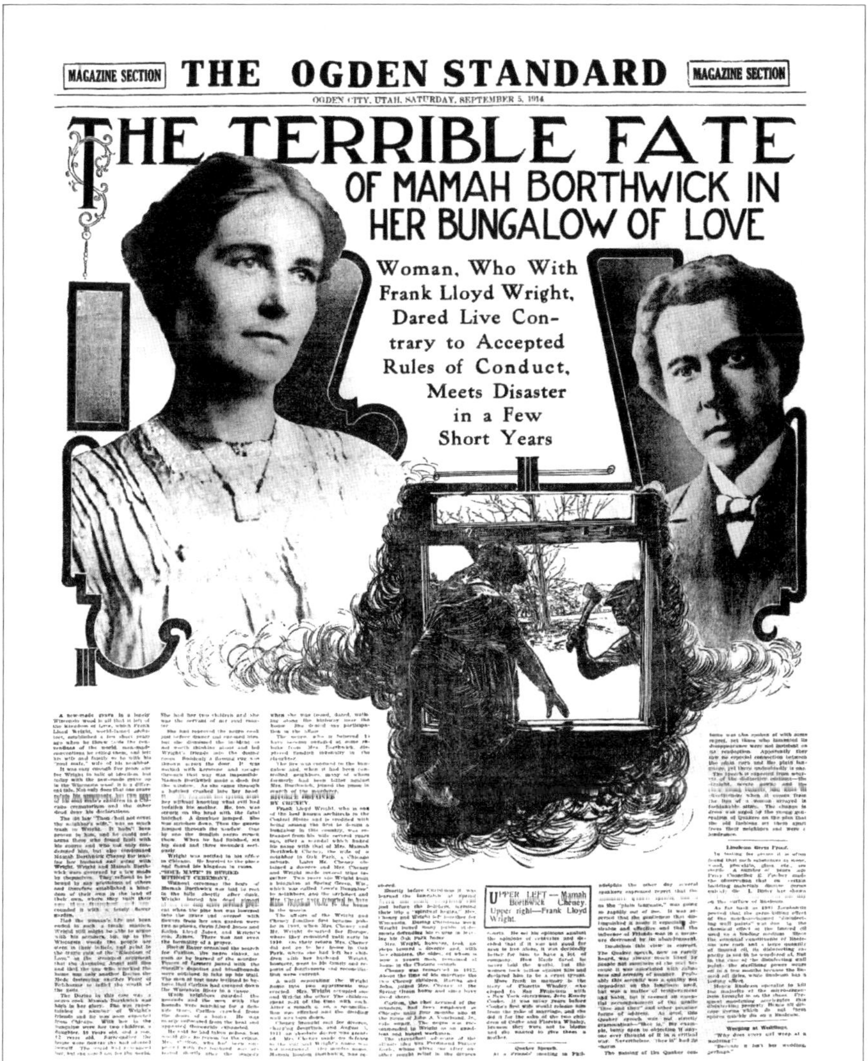
MAGAZINE SECTION THE OGDEN STANDARD MAGAZINE SECTION

OGDEN CITY, UTAH, SATURDAY, SEPTEMBER 5, 1914

THE TERRIBLE FATE OF MAMAH BORTHWICK IN HER BUNGALOW OF LOVE

Woman, Who With Frank Lloyd Wright, Dared Live Contrary to Accepted Rules of Conduct, Meets Disaster in a Few Short Years

UPPER LEFT — Mamah Borthwick Cheney. Upper right—Frank Lloyd Wright.

Front page of the magazine section of the *Ogden Standard* (Ogden City, Utah), on September 4, 1914, describing the murders at Taliesin.

into the grave in solitude. There was no tombstone at the time. "Why mark the spot," he later wrote, "where desolation ended and began?"[90]

Looking back at that catastrophic episode in Wright's life, there is no way to reconstruct—or to begin to imagine—his state of mind and the bewildering surge of emotions he felt.

As Brendan Gill, one of Wright's biographers, wrote, it is not often that we pass, in a brief span of hours, "from the happiest moments of one's life to the most despairing."[91]

2

MASON CITY MEETS MODERN DESIGN

However vast the distance—let alone the cultural gap—between London, England, and Mason City, Iowa, 1851 was a consequential year for both.

Iowa had been granted statehood in 1846. But it was not until five years later that Cerro Gordo County was founded by Euro-American settlers and their immigrant families, who constructed makeshift cabins near the present community of Clear Lake. The closest other settlements of white immigrants were fifty miles east in Chickasaw County.

Mason City is nine miles east of Clear Lake. Initially known by various names (Shibboleth, Masonic Grove, and Masonville), it was officially established in 1853. Before the end of the decade, it had become the county seat.[92]

At mid-century, the area's white settlers had largely tranquil dealings with small bands of Native Americans who had traditionally summered near Clear Lake. When occasional violence did break out, it typically occurred between indigenous hostile nations, fueled by old, unsettled scores.

In the early 1850s, area settlers vacated the area briefly in response to events that were generally known as the Grindstone War. But of far greater concern was the killing by Native Americans in 1857 of about forty white settlers at Spirit Lake, Iowa (known by whites as the Spirit Lake Massacre), one hundred miles west of Mason City.[93]

Despite such setbacks, in an effort to encourage continued settlement, the U.S. government declared the area a neutral zone, open to white settlers but off limits to Native American groups.

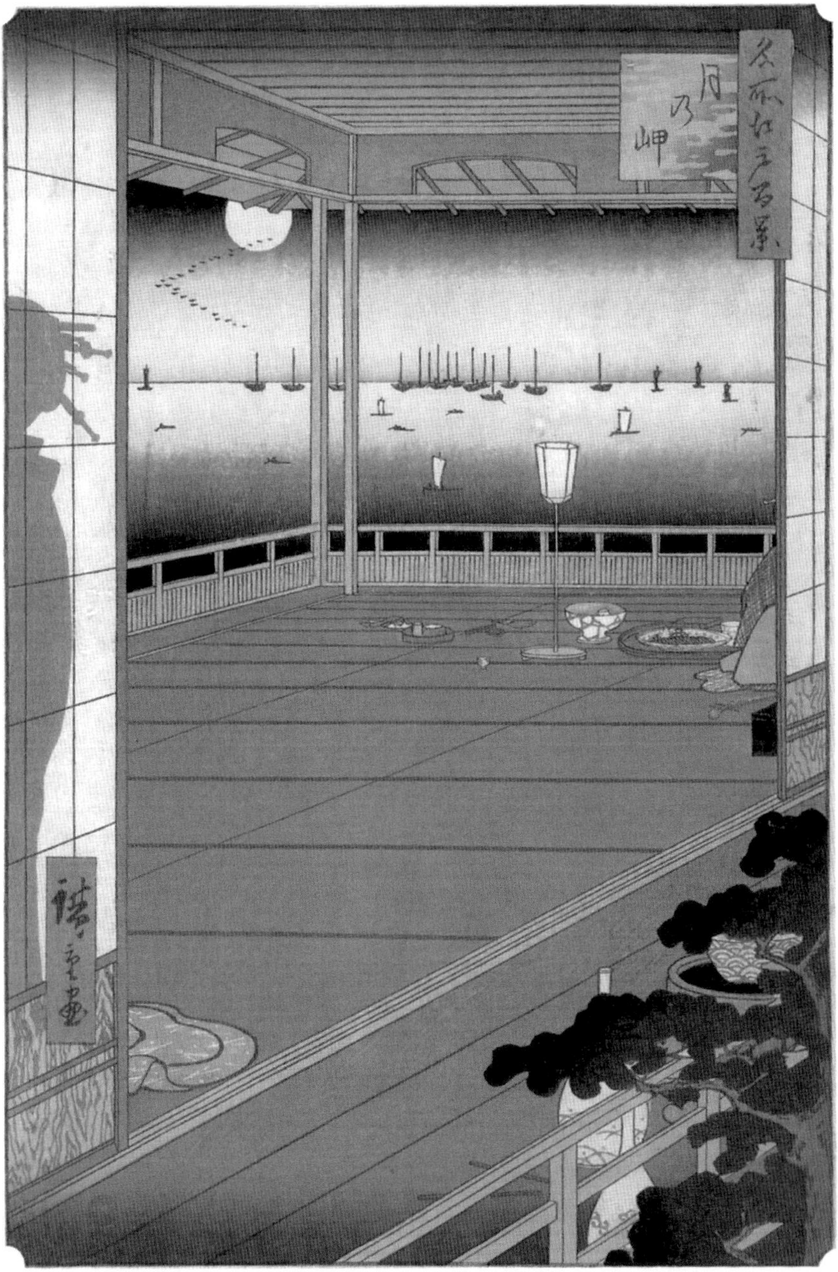

Ukiyo-e woodblock print, titled *Moon-Viewing Point*, by Utagawa Hiroshige (circa 1857). *LOC Prints and Photographs.*

Predictably, the infusion of settlers continued, and by 1860, there were 940 Euro-Americans in Cerro Gordo County alone and, a decade later, nearly 5,000.

During the second half of the nineteenth century, as the population increased, the county and its residents were inextricably overwhelmed by the effects of the Industrial Revolution, which had begun in the previous century in England and other regions of Europe.

Before they knew what hit them, residents of Cerro Gordo County were profoundly and irreversibly changed by a torrent of innovation in manufacturing, transportation, communication, agriculture, finance, building materials—and architecture.

Industrial Revolution

In London, England, more than four thousand miles east of Mason City, the changes that took place in 1851 were even more momentous. It marked the opening of the first World's Fair, an occasion officially titled the Great Exhibition of the Works of Industry of All Nations.[94]

Of lasting effect both culturally and economically, the fair was the first concerted attempt to promote industrial products to potential investors and buyers, as well as an opportunity for other countries to demonstrate their own achievements.

That first World's Fair was also important architecturally because of the building in which it was housed. Erected temporarily in Hyde Park in central London, it was open to the public only from May to mid-October that year. A two-story, massive, eighteen-acre iron-and-glass enclosure, it was the world's largest building at the time.

Designed by architect Joseph Paxton, an expert on botanical gardens, the building was essentially a gargantuan greenhouse, which explains why pundits called it the "Crystal Palace," a name that caught on with the public as well. When the fair ended, the structure was dismantled, and its components were reassembled (in modified form) at Sydenham, a suburb of London, where it functioned for many years as a generic events center.

At the Hyde Park Crystal Palace, about fourteen thousand exhibits were shown. Just to walk through the exhibits was a distance of eight miles or more. The majority of items were sponsored by the British. But there were also notable entries from other countries, including the United States, among

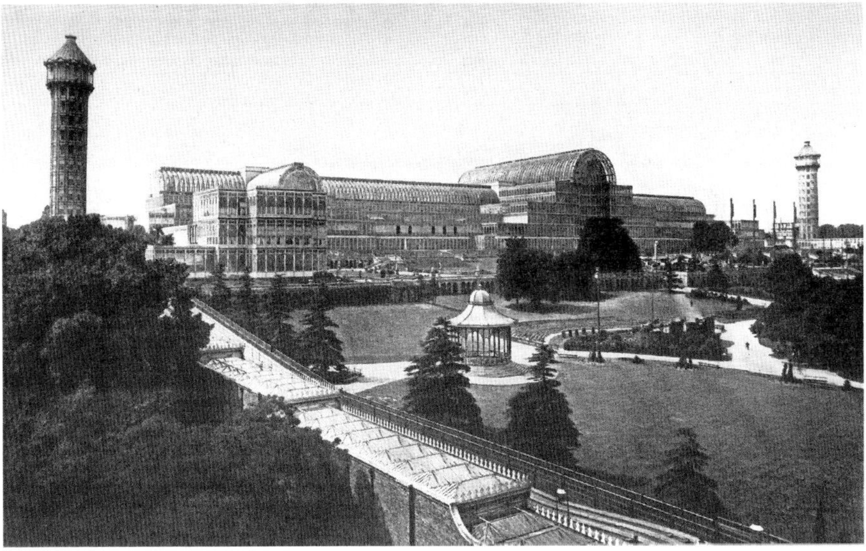

The Crystal Palace was essentially an eighteen-acre greenhouse made of machine-manufactured components. *Vintage postcard.*

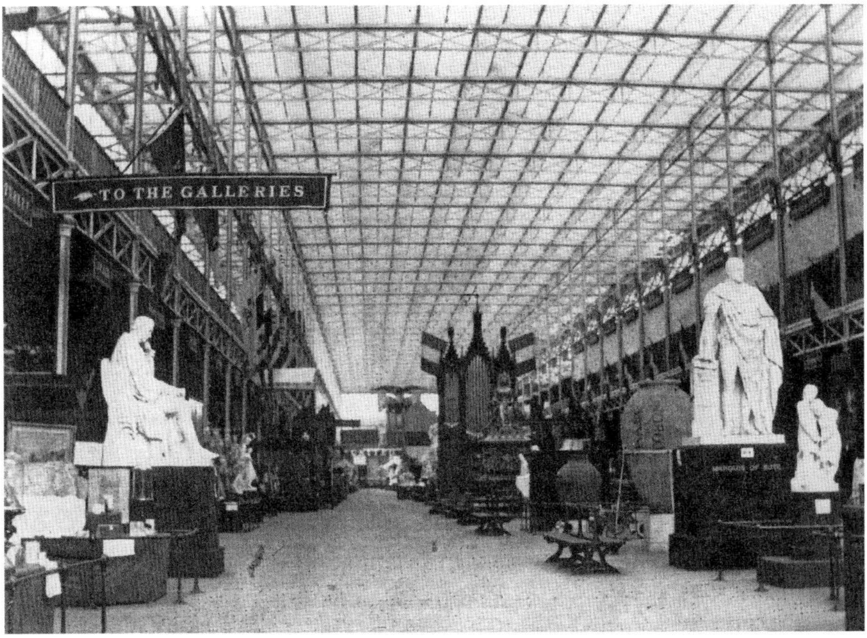

Interior view (detail) of the Crystal Palace (1851). Public domain.

whose most popular products were McCormick's reaper, the Colt revolver, Goodyear rubber products, reliable false teeth and chewing tobacco.

At the time, no one could have anticipated the success of the Crystal Palace, economic and otherwise. Queen Victoria loved it (and not just because it was the pet project of her husband, Prince Albert). She visited the fair at least three times, noting in her letters that it included every conceivable invention and was "incredibly glorious, really like fairyland."[95]

In the end, the exhibition was attended by more than six million visitors (three times the population of London at the time), each of whom paid for admission. A financial loss had been anticipated, but it made an astonishing profit instead, which then led to a clamorous rush by other countries to host the next industrial fair.

Innovative Forerunner

It is often claimed that the Crystal Palace was a forerunner of modernism in architecture because of its building innovations (not for the gaudy kitsch products inside). It is even commonly said to have been the first Modern building for features we take for granted today.

For example, it was made of what we now regard as "modern" building materials—glass and iron—although the floor was made of wood. Its components were machine made, not handcrafted. Further, those same parts were mass produced in various factories and then transported to Hyde Park to be put together by workers at the site. The cast-iron and plate glass components were modular and standardized, as is the usual practice today.

Other features were early attempts at aligning form with function, as would later be championed by Chicago architect Louis H. Sullivan. As is well known, he would be the mentor of some of the leading Prairie School architects, including those who contributed to Mason City architecture, the most famous being Frank Lloyd Wright.

One of the problems encountered in designing the Crystal Palace was the preservation of ancient trees in Hyde Park. British politicians insisted that certain historic elms be spared so that the park could return to its earlier state after the fair had ended.

As a solution, Paxton preserved the living trees by including them inside the building—the walls were built around them. (Not surprisingly, there was a problem with sparrows inside—an issue that could be easily solved, someone suggested, by the addition of sparrow hawks.)

In this, and by using glass for the walls (through which one could see outside), the building was an early attempt at blurring the rigid distinctions between inside and outside or, as Wright would later say, at dissolving the boxlike confines of the house.

There was no electrical lighting in 1851, so how could there be adequate light in which to view the exhibits? As it turned out, natural lighting proved sufficient because the building was made of glass.

But that, in itself, caused a problem because the sunlight, in addition to the body heat of thousands of visitors, raised the interior temperature. Paxton's solution was to install external adjustable shades, which were sprayed with water. He also used rudimentary air conditioning, produced by circulating air that rose up through intentional gaps in the floor.[96]

The Crystal Palace was an ingenious early attempt to address various issues that are now part and parcel of building design. Looking back, it truly did anticipate some of the innovative practices that would later be more fully explored by Sullivan, Wright and other modern-era architects—including those who contributed to Mason City's City National Bank, Park Inn Hotel and the Rock Crest/Rock Glen neighborhood.

Grammar of Architecture

Not everyone praised the Crystal Palace, in part because a lot of the things on exhibit were blatantly wasteful and overwrought. But there were other features that were genuinely functional, thoughtful and educational.

Among these were the Fine Art Courts, consisting of examples of design and architecture from exotic times and cultures, including courts devoted to Nineveh, Egyptian, Alhambra, Medieval, Renaissance, Italian and Pompeian traditions, among others.

The design of these was overseen by Owen Jones, a Welsh architect, who also determined the entire inside arrangement of the Crystal Palace and chose the building's color scheme.[97]

Five years after the World's Fair (by which time the building had reopened at Sydenham), Jones published an elaborate chromo-lithographic book called *The Grammar of Ornament*, which became a standard source book for historic styles worldwide.[98]

This book was published in 1856, the year that also marked the birth of Louis Sullivan. It would prove indispensable to architectural training, thanks to its 150 color plates and the persuasive clarity of its text.

With the publication of *The Grammar of Ornament*, it would be another eleven years before the birth of Frank Lloyd Wright, and a half century in advance of the *Wasmuth Portfolio* in Berlin.

In Jones's book, there is an introduction called "General Principles in the Arrangement of Form and Color in Architecture and the Decorative Arts." It includes thirty-seven design principles or propositions, many of which anticipated the architectural best practices that Wright and others would later promote.[99]

In his autobiography, Wright recalled having been influenced by Jones's *Grammar of Ornament*, a copy of which he initially found in the library of his uncle Jenk's All Souls Church in Chicago.[100]

Among the book's propositions is the recommendation that various visual components (motifs or rhyming attributes), such as certain proportions, colors, textures or angles, should occur repeatedly in a design so that "the whole and each particular part should be a multiple of some simple unit."[101]

Throughout his life, Frank Lloyd Wright used a comparable method in his own building designs, which he described as the "grammar" of a building. Most likely, it was Jones's book that encouraged Wright to use the phrase "the grammar of architecture."

As Wright later wrote:

> *Every house worth considering as a work of art must have a grammar of its own. "Grammar," in this sense, means the same thing in any construction—whether it be of words or of stone or wood. It is the shape-relationship between the various elements that enter into the constitution of the thing. The "grammar" of the house is its manifest articulation of all its parts. ...Consistency in grammar is therefore the property—solely—of a well-developed artist-architect.*[102]

Edgar Tafel, who was Wright's apprentice for almost a decade, recalled how recurrent components were used ("down to the smallest details") in Wright's design of the Darwin D. Martin House in Buffalo, New York. "For the Martin house," wrote Tafel,

> *Mr. Wright used one kind of brick outside, so he used the same brick on the inside...In keeping with the grammar, the tile of the floor of the exterior*

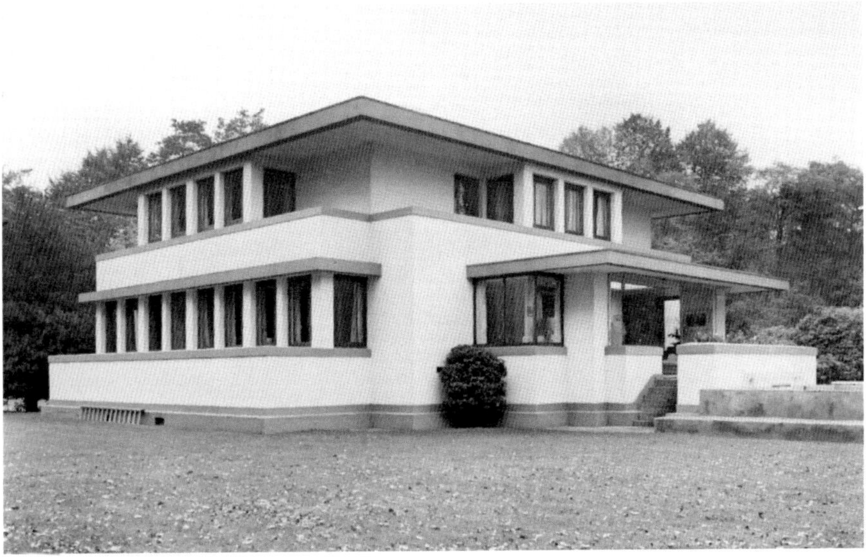

Villa Henny, designed in 1915–19 by Robert Van 't Hoff, near Utrecht, the Netherlands. Note its resemblance to Prairie School homes. *Photograph by Rijksdienst voor Cultureel Erfgoed (Wikimedia Commons).*

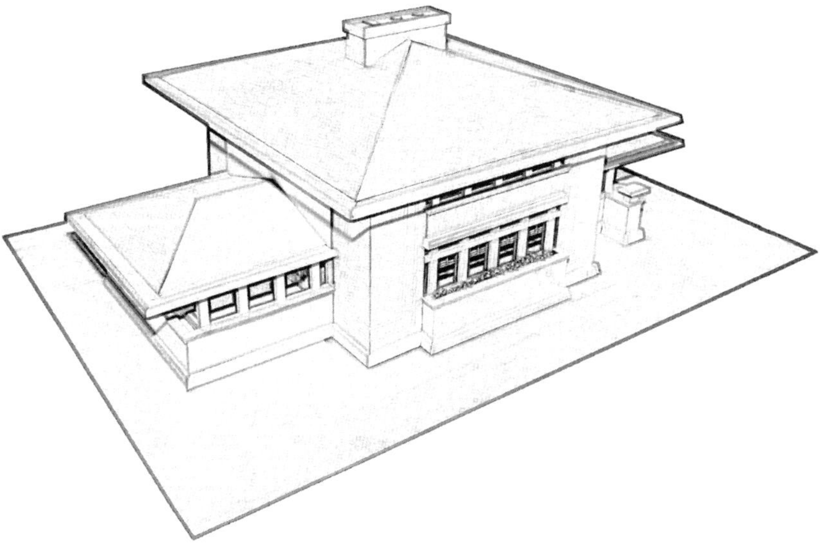

The Stockman House in Mason City, as seen in a model at the Robert E. McCoy Architectural Interpretive Center. *Digital drawing from author's photograph.*

> *porch was the same as the tile on the floor inside. He used only one kind of plaster—sand-floated with integral color. And only one kind of wood: oak. The chairs and the tables were oak and so was all the wood trim. The total feeling of the house was of one stripe, from the overall plan down to the furniture, the door jambs, and the window frames.*[103]

It was Wright's belief that a comparable grammar is no less critical in works of art (as, for example, in paintings) than it is in building design. He was not alone in that belief, as exemplified by two paintings by midwestern artists Thomas Hart Benton and Grant Wood, whose working years converged with Wright's. Among their best-known artworks are, respectively, *Achelous and Hercules* and *American Gothic.*

How Form Functions

When *Achelous and Hercules* (1947) is viewed not only as a pictorial allegory but also more generally as an arrangement of shapes, sizes, lines, colors, angles and other structural attributes, it is clear that it is built around a rhythmic recurrence of features.

Among its achievements is an informal balance of colors. But there are also intricate shape-based rhymes, two in particular: (1) an oval or elliptical shape (a circle in perspective) and (2) a serpentine or whip-like shape.

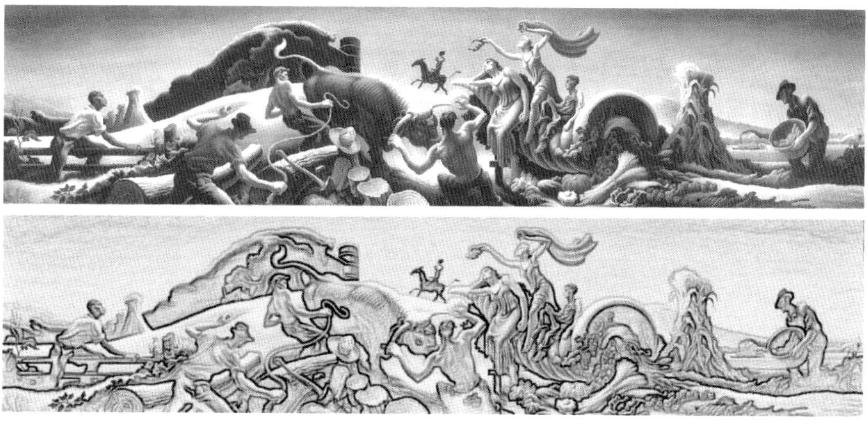

Painting by Thomas Hart Benton, *Achelous and Hercules* (1947). *Wikimedia Commons (with author's diagram).*

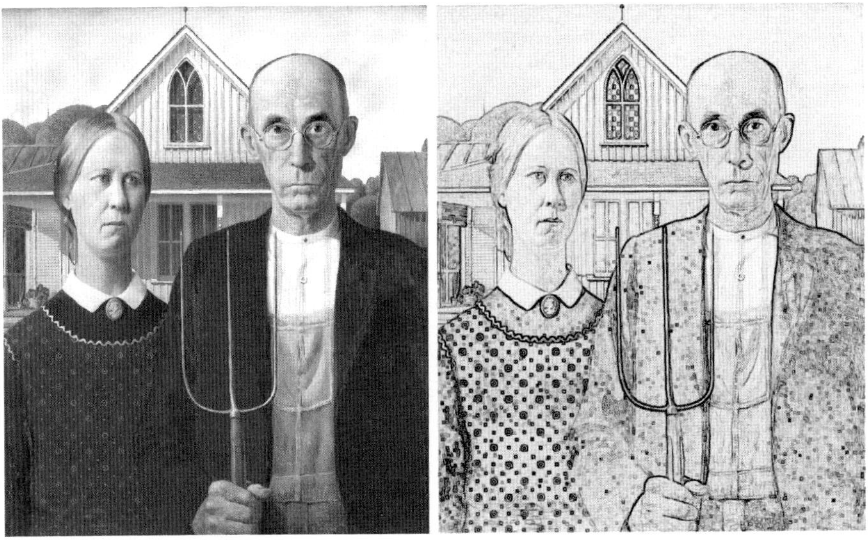

Painting by Grant Wood, *American Gothic* (1930). *Wikimedia Commons (with author's diagram).*

As is shown by a diagram of that painting, these shapes occur repeatedly, but each time in a new disguise. Sometimes, the serpentine line appears in the form of a rope; the tail of a bull; an axe handle; the tail of a horse in the background; the outstretched arm of a woman, as well as the windblown scarf she holds; the smoke from a steamboat; and so on. The second, elliptical shape can be found in the rim of the bushel basket on the right, the mouth of the horn of plenty, the tops of the severed tree stumps, the brim of the hat in the foreground and so on.

In Grant Wood's *American Gothic* (1930), it is equally apparent that a comparable method was used. Wood's painting is a visual pun, a cartoon-like portrayal of the beliefs and attitudes of midwestern Euro-Americans (among them those who colonized Cerro Gordo County), compared to the houses in which they reside.

The painting's title might have been *We Are What We Live In*. The house in the background is typical of a then-prevalent architectural style called Carpenter Gothic. Among its standard features is an upright vertical gesture (derived from the worshipful upward thrust of Gothic cathedrals), abetted by tall, thin windows. These are the same paired verticals that occur famously in the arches of the Brooklyn Bridge, in side-by-side vertical windows and in patterned, stripe-like vertical slats (called board and batten siding) in Gothic-style houses.

In that rich architectural context, the artist has placed in the foreground another pair of uprights: two thin, dutiful Euro-Americans (a farmer and his daughter, according to Wood). Their frontally centered stalwart pose is an intentional echo of the same double *U* in the three-pronged fork the farmer holds (in a preparatory thumbnail sketch, Wood had initially chosen a rake), the *U*-shaped stitched motif on the bib of the man's overalls and, more quietly, the exaggerated facial philtrims (the vertical indentation between the upper lip and nose) to strengthen the side-by-side symmetry of the human face.

In Grant Wood's paintings, form and content (or form and function, if you will) work in tandem. In *American Gothic*, the recurrence of that double *U* reinforces Wood's portrayal of his subjects' "righteous" bearing (his term), the rigidity of their strait-laced (corseted) lives and the belief that a God-fearing Euro-American should focus first and foremost on the quest for everlasting, heavenly peace—which they assumed was in the sky.

Like Wood and Benton and their contemporaries, Frank Lloyd Wright had grown up in the shadow of the Gothic Revival (as famously promoted by British art critic John Ruskin and designer William Morris), which was gradually transformed into the arts and crafts movement. He was well acquainted with the enchantment of uplifting gestures (church steeples among them) that might divert parishioners from the ordeals of daily life on earth.

But he was also profoundly committed to transcendentalism and Unitarianism, which emphasized the unity of all things, as well as the omnipresence of God—diffuse and attendant at all times.

EMBRACING THE PRAIRIE

In 1904, when Wright was proposing to design Unity Temple, the church's leader had assumed that (as with other churches) it would, of course, be crowned by a steeple. In reply to which Wright asked, "Why point to heaven?" Why use the steeple's "finger" (his term) to misdirect attention away from experiential life on earth?[104]

A genuine encounter with God, with "God's countenance," said Wright, is far more likely to be found in the parishioners of the church themselves.

Like other architects of the same era, Wright made powerful use of uprights, especially in his early career. But as he moved toward the Prairie School phase of his architectural career, he increasingly used exaggerated verticals, not for the overall shape of the house, but instead for interior details (called accents), including elongated ladder-back or tall-back side chairs for

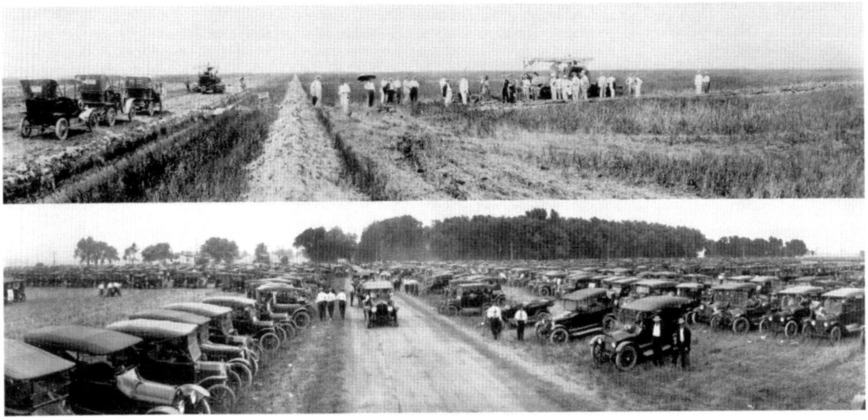

Two panoramic photographs of the flat midwestern prairie (circa 1910). *LOC Prints and Photographs.*

dining room furniture or vertical stripe-like patterns of wood in interior trim and elsewhere.

As is widely known, Wright was increasingly drawn to the extraordinary flatness of the midwestern prairie—"the gently rolling or level prairies of our great Middle West," he said, "where every detail of elevation becomes exaggerated."[105]

At the same time, he did not completely abandon the Gothic upright; instead, he turned it on its side so that it embraced the prairie instead of reaching for the sky. As often as not, that expansive wing-spread form became a cantilevered plane, as in the ledge-like concrete slabs of his design for Fallingwater.

As Wright scholar Donald Hoffmann said, "Wright effectively turned the Gothic on end. His horizontal rhythms told the truth of things by expressing the repose of masses in harmony with gravity and the landscape; his architecture spoke of life here and now, not the kingdom of a Christian heaven."[106]

Quest for Oil

As noted earlier, the community that would become known as Mason City, Iowa, was established in 1853. By coincidence, it was in that very same year that another primary influence in Wright's life also took place (still more than a decade before he was born).

That critical event occurred more than ninety thousand miles west of Mason City in the harbor of Tokyo, Japan, where a half century later Wright would be commissioned to design the Imperial Hotel.

What happened in Tokyo Bay in 1853 had everything to do with the Industrial Revolution—as well as with the eventual growth of Cerro Gordo County and Mason City. Three years earlier, California had achieved statehood, which enabled the U.S. government to set up West Coast shipping ports. This set the stage for permanent trade relationships with Pacific nations, while relying less on American ports on the East Coast.[107]

Not surprisingly, all this was related to oil—not petroleum but whale oil. Whale oil was highly valued at the time for its use in machine lubrication, soap and margarine, as well as a lantern fuel. Also of value was whale bone, the uses of which (in corsets, collar stays, eyeglass frames and other products) foretold the need for plastics.

Unfortunately, whales had been hunted in excess off the coast of New England (remember Melville's *Moby Dick*), creating an urgent need for new whale-hunting options in the Pacific, combined with other resources.

To complicate matters, there was a critical problem because Japan's shipping ports had been tightly closed to foreigners (even diplomatic envoys) since the 1630s.

But in 1853, U.S. commodore Matthew Perry sailed abruptly into Tokyo Bay with four heavily armed steamships and (threatening to attack) delivered a letter from President Millard Fillmore, demanding trade negotiations. Perry then departed but returned early the following year, with twice the number of armed, ominous black ships. This time, Japan agreed to open its ports.

In subsequent years, the consequences not only benefited Japanese and Western commerce but also led to a frenzy of interest among Europeans and Americans in Japanese cultural artifacts (prints, ceramics, furniture, clothing, fans and so on). For the rest of the nineteenth century and into the twentieth, Westerners all but went berserk in a strange collecting frenzy for traditional Japanese products.

This whirlwind phenomenon, which the French called *Japonisme*, was affiliated with art styles like impressionism, the aesthetic movement, art nouveau (derived from the name of a gallery in Paris, owned by Siegfried Bing, where imported Japanese items were exhibited and sold) and the arts and crafts movement.[108]

The widest assortment of Western artists, designers and architects was captivated by the quaintness and startling simplicity of Japanese artifacts. They were especially interested in a category of woodblock prints known as Ukiyo-e, or "Pictures of the Floating World" (a euphemism for the red-light district).

Those influenced by these prints included James A.M. Whistler, Henri de Toulouse-Lautrec, Mary Cassatt, Pierre Bonnard, Édouard Manet, Paul Gauguin, Claude Monet, Charles Rennie Mackintosh, Edvard Munch and Alphonse Mucha, to name a few.

An especially avid enthusiast was Vincent Van Gogh, who made interpretations of some of the Ukiyo-e prints as oil paintings or showed them hanging on the walls in the backgrounds of his paintings of room interiors. In a letter in 1888, Van Gogh told his brother that "all my work is in a way founded on Japanese art…"[109]

But there were other consequences as well, among them Whistler's *The Peacock Room*, Gilbert and Sullivan's *The Mikado* and the exotic illustrations of Aubrey Beardsley.

Japanese Prints

In the meantime, Western familiarity with Japanese artifacts was greatly accelerated by their inclusion in international trade exhibitions, including those in London in 1862 and in Paris in 1867 and 1878. Japanese prints were also shown at the 1876 Centennial International Exhibition in Philadelphia, where other innovations were the Remington typewriter, Shaker furniture, Hires root beer, Heinz ketchup, Alexander Graham Bell's telephone, bananas, popcorn and even kudzu (to counter soil erosion).

As mentioned earlier, it was the same exposition that included a kindergarten demonstration, which Frank Lloyd Wright's mother attended and which prompted her to buy a set of Froebel blocks for her preteen son, the aspiring architect. This is noteworthy because young Frank would soon become a major collector, dealer and curator of Ukiyo-e prints.

It is important to reiterate that whenever Wright was asked what had influenced his development as an architect, he invariably cited two factors. One was his childhood introduction to Froebel's kindergarten blocks, and the other was his long-term interest in Japanese prints.

In his autobiography, Wright said that "if Japanese prints were to be deducted from my education, I don't know what direction the whole might have taken."[110]

And in an address to his apprentices in 1957, he recalled that when he saw Japanese prints for the first time, "and I saw the elimination of the insignificant and simplicity of vision, together with the sense of rhythm and the importance of design, I began to see nature in a totally different way."[111]

So what was it about Ukiyo-e woodblock prints that made them so enchanting to Wright, as well as to so many others in art, architecture and design?

There are many ways to answer that (all of them both interesting and complex), but of particular relevance here is that these prints were made in accordance with an underlying structural plan comprising geometric shapes. It may help to think back to the earlier examples of the paintings of Benton and Wood, both of whom were well aware of Ukiyo-e woodblock prints.

One of the first to talk about this was an American artist, author and art educator named Arthur Wesley Dow. One of Dow's followers, Alon Bement, was an important teacher for Georgia O'Keeffe, while another, Ernest Batchelder, was Grant Wood's design instructor. In 1899, Dow published an influential book titled *Composition: A Series of Exercises in Art Structure for the Use of Students and Teachers*. It went through many editions, and although the text is outdated now, it remains in print today.[112]

Compositional Framework

Kakuzo Okakura, a Japanese scholar who was Dow's friend and Asian counterpart (and the author of a famous book called *The Book of Tea*) referred to these structural lines as "bones," in the sense of framework or skeletal plans.[113]

But Dow himself preferred the phrase "line ideas." To him, they were equally fundamental in art, architecture and design.

> *Each* [whether artist or designer] *has before him* [when he starts] *a blank space on which he sketches out the main lines of his composition. This may be called his line-idea, and on it hinges the excellence of the whole...A picture, then, may be said to be in its beginning actually a pattern of lines.*[114]

In Dow's book, he illustrates this concept with side-by-side illustrations, in the first of which two vertical trees are represented, with other features in the background, positioned horizontally.

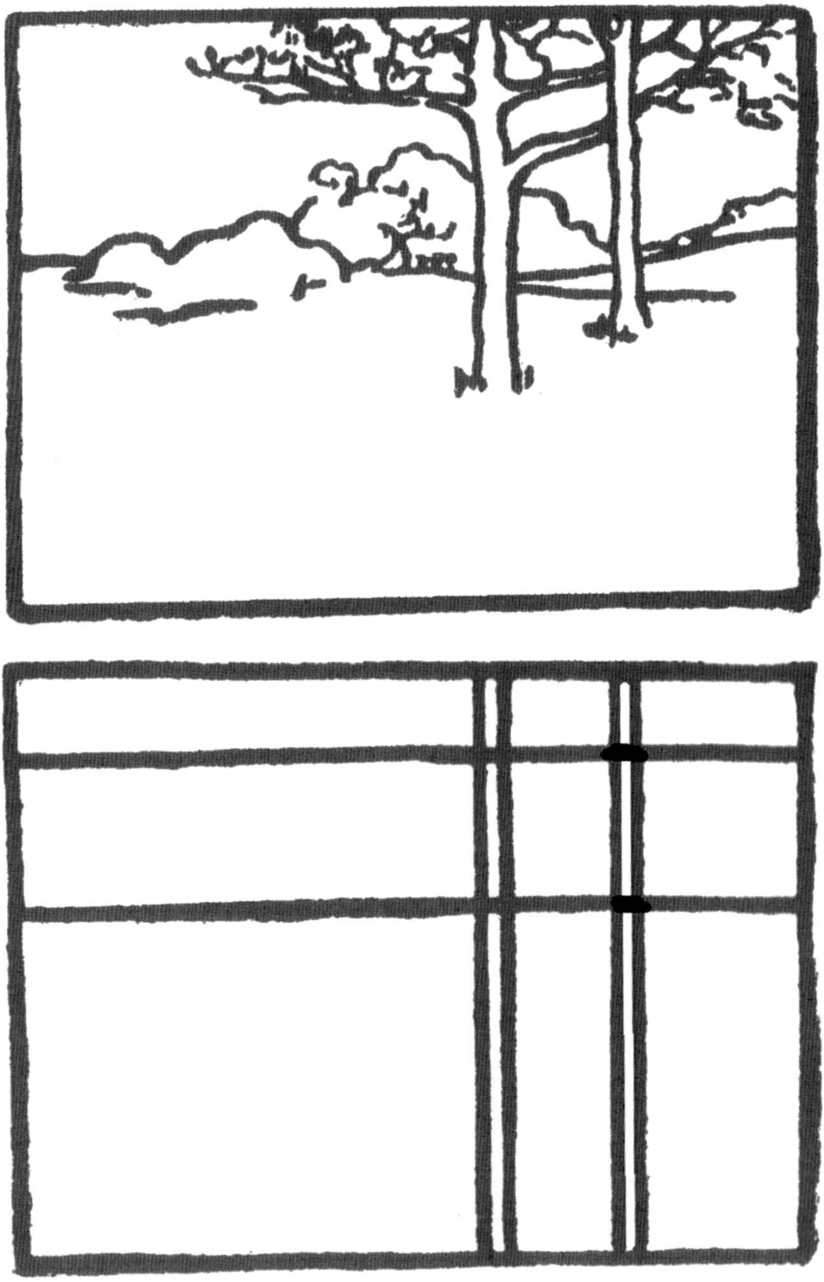

Drawing and diagram from Arthur Wesley Dow's *Composition* (1899), showing the underlying line idea in a drawing of two trees.

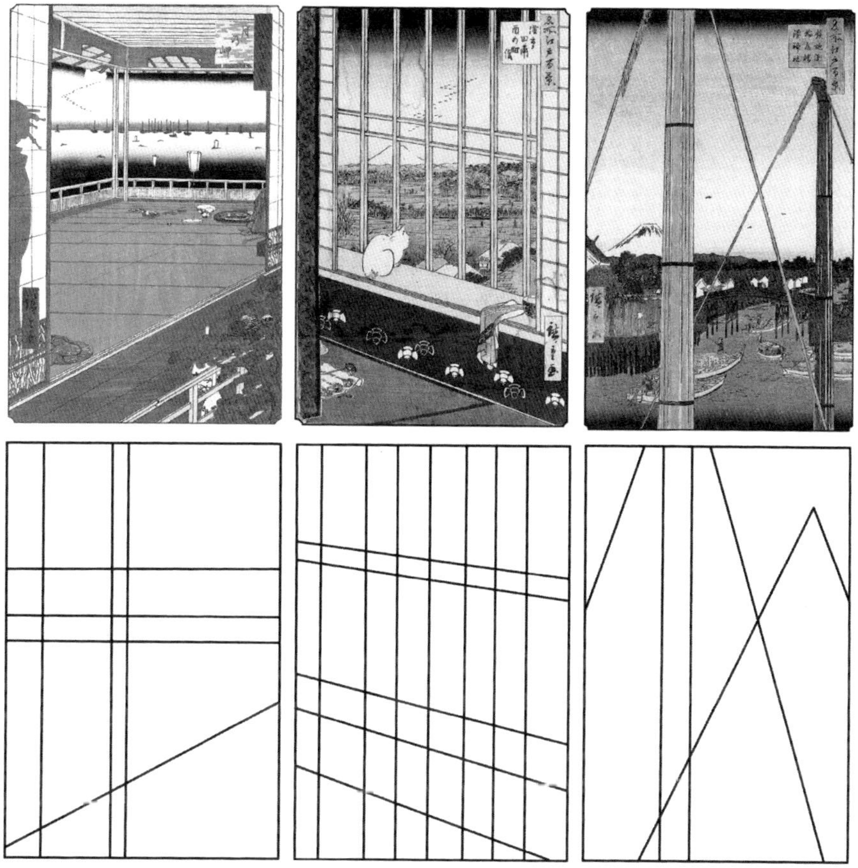

Comparable analyses of three woodblock prints by Ando Hiroshige. *LOC Prints and Photographs (with author's diagrams).*

The second is a diagram (the initial line idea) of the underlying structure for the same composition, composed of "an arrangement of rectangular spaces much like the gingham [or tartan or plaid] and other simple patterns."[115]

While Dow may have coined the term "line idea," he was not the first to use underlying structural plans in art and design compositions. Equivalent methods had been used for centuries, and today (because of our use of computers), they are used more widely than ever before.

They are no longer known as line ideas but are instead referred to as "grid lines" or "layout grids." For example, nearly every publication today (books, magazines, newspapers, brochures, posters and websites) is based on an invisible network of lines (of which most readers are unaware), in part because virtually all publication design software provides default layout grids, which can either be activated or turned off.

Why are grid lines widely used? Simply, it is because of how our brains are built: as proposed by gestalt psychologists and confirmed by current neuroscience, we have an inherent tendency (a perceptual default) to see as belonging together shapes that are lined up in space, sometimes called "edge alignment."

That's why rows and columns in a marching band appear to move together as one. That's why we indent for paragraph breaks. Simply, these are reliably powerful ways to make a composition appear orderly (whether page designs or building plans)—to make it easier to navigate.[116]

Reproduced here are diagrams of two well-known paintings from the late nineteenth and early twentieth centuries. One, titled *Arrangement in Gray and Black No. 1: The Artist's Mother* (1871–72), is by American expatriate artist James A.M. Whistler; the other, called *Portrait of Fritza Riedler* (1906), is by Vienna secessionist painter Gustav Klimt.

Both artists were strongly influenced by Japanese prints. Whistler was about thirty years older than Klimt, and there is nearly the same span of time between the completion of their two paintings. The artists were well acquainted, and Klimt admired Whistler's work. Surely, it is not a mere coincidence that the two paintings have such similar layouts. More than likely, Klimt's painting was a tacit, deliberate tribute to Whistler.

Like artists and graphic designers, architects have often used edge alignment to make distinct components appear to connect. In addition, they have also lined up focal points in a method that architect Le Corbusier called "regulating lines."[117]

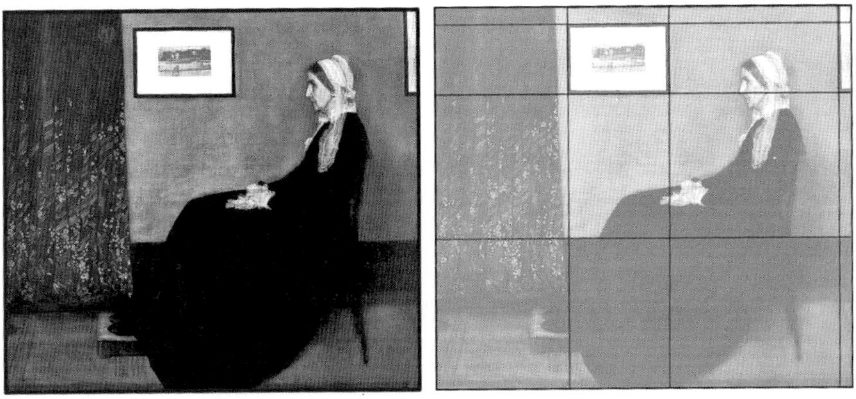

Arrangement in Gray and Black No. 1: The Artist's Mother (1871–72) by James A.M. Whistler. *Wikimedia Commons (with author's diagram).*

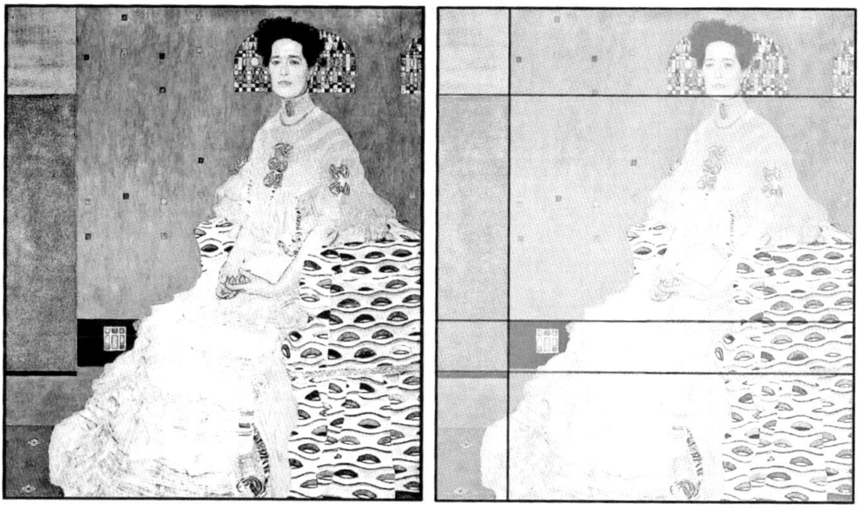

Portrait of Fritza Riedler (1906) by Gustav Klimt. *Wikimedia Commons (with author's diagram).*

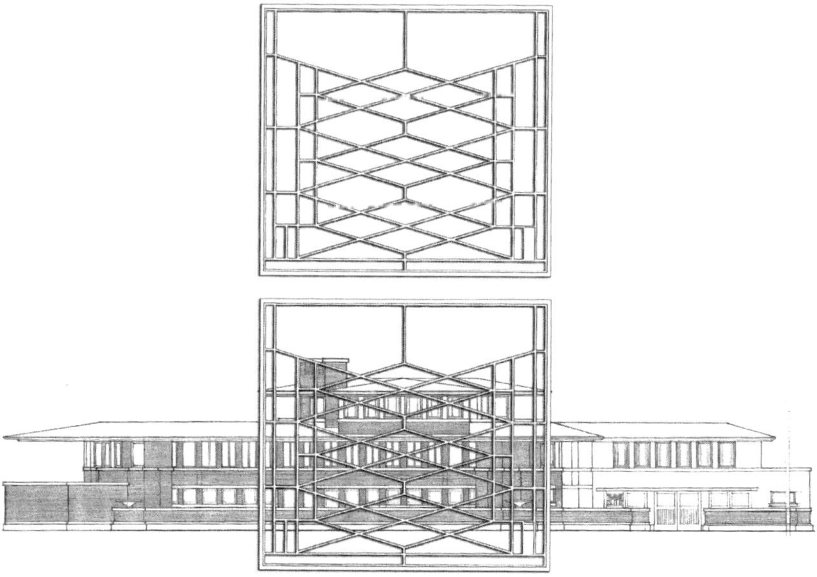

Comparison of art glass window and building design for the Robie House, as proposed by Jonathan Hale. *Historic American Buildings Survey, LOC Prints and Photographs (with author's diagram).*

There is a vivid discussion of this in *The Old Way of Seeing* by architect Jonathan Hale. "The most common type of regulating line," he writes, "is a diagonal connecting key points on a rectangle...but they can [also] be circles or semicircles."[118]

Of the visual examples cited by Hale, perhaps the most astonishing is an architectural drawing of the south elevation of the Robie House by Frank Lloyd Wright, juxtaposed for comparison with an art glass window from the same building.[119] As our own revision of that diagram shows, the grammar in the window's line idea is echoed by the pattern in the profile of the building.

Indebtedness to Japanese

The origin of this kind of grammar may be, as Wright himself explained,

> *some plant form that has appealed to me, as certain properties in line and form of the sumac were used in the Lawrence house at Springfield; but in every case the motif is adhered to throughout so that...each building aesthetically is cut from one piece of goods and consistently hangs together with an integrity impossible otherwise.*[120]

In comparing Dow's line ideas with diagrams of woodblock prints, it is obvious that all of these might readily have functioned as plans for art glass windows—especially when abstracted to the degree of those designed by Wright.

As David Hanks has noted, plant-based motifs are commonly found in the work of other turn-of-the-century designers, but "none carried the designs to the extreme geometric abstraction or the 'essence of the plant' that Wright did in his art glass."[121]

Or, as Joseph Masheck writes, some of Dow's line idea diagrams "compare respectably with such productions...as stained-glass windows...by Frank Lloyd Wright."[122]

It is plausible that Dow's influence on Wright's architectural compositions may have been more direct than that. In 1893, Dow had been appointed a curator of the Japanese art collection at the Boston Museum of Fine Arts, where he was strongly influenced by an eminent Asian scholar, Ernest Fenollosa, who was the head curator of the same collection. Fenollosa's

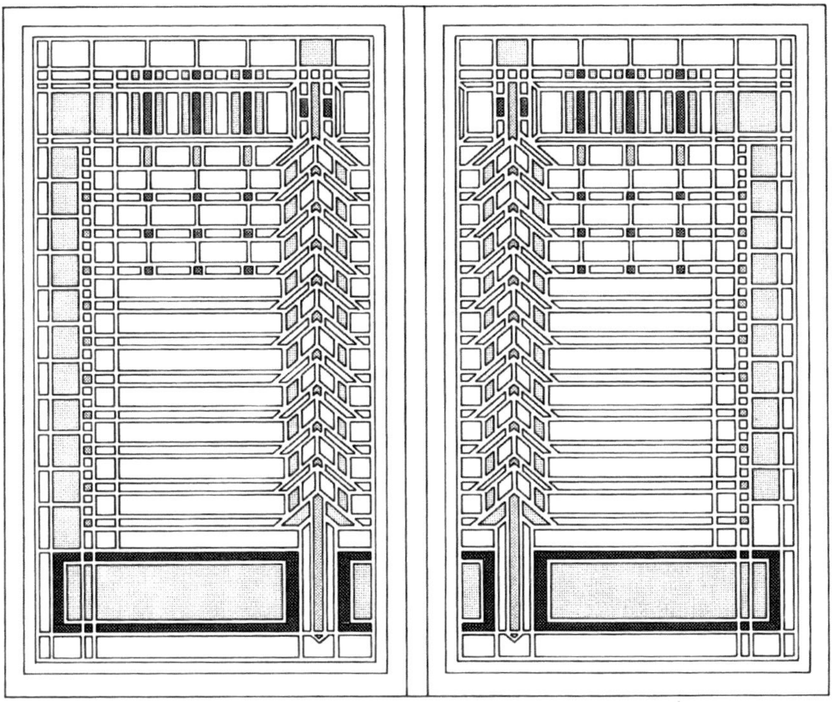

This page: Examples of Wright's art glass window designs for the Darwin Martin House. *Historic American Buildings Survey, LOC Prints and Photographs.*

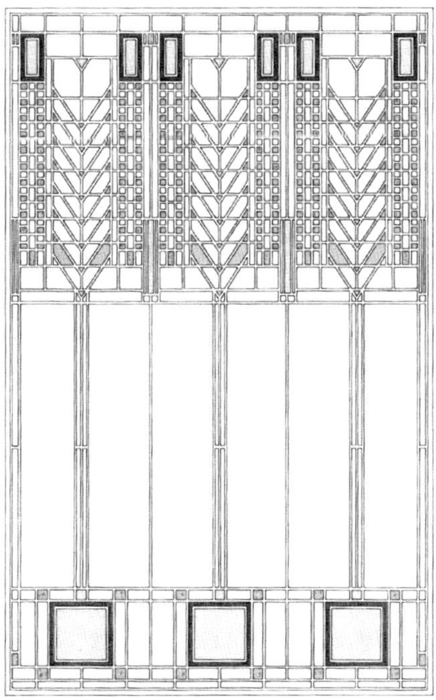

mother was Mary Silsbee, and his first cousin was a Chicago-based architect named Joseph Lyman Silsbee.[123]

Interestingly, in 1886, it was Silsbee who was hired to design a chapel (called Unity Chapel) near Spring Green for none other than the Lloyd Jones family, Frank Lloyd Wright's Unitarian clan. That same year, Wright dropped out of the University of Wisconsin and joined the staff of Silsbee's firm. In that office, he was surely introduced to Ukiyo-e woodblock prints (given by Fenollosa to Silsbee, his cousin) and may have begun his own collection in 1890.[124]

As historian Kevin Nute has persuasively shown, it is likely that some of Dow's line ideas—whether consciously or not—were initial inspirations for the floor plans of some of Wright's residential designs.[125] It is also suggested that Wright was influenced by Japanese architecture (not just Ukiyo-e prints), despite his repeated denials.

In that regard, he was especially offended when his friend Charles Ashbee, the British Arts and Crafts designer, stated (and refused to edit out) in the introduction to the second volume of the *Wasmuth Portfolio* that there was a "very clear" Japanese influence in Wright's architecture. "He is obviously trying to adapt Japanese forms to the United States," Ashbee continued, "even though the artist denies it and the influence must be unconscious."[126]

To that statement, Wright replied (in a letter to Ashbee), "Do not accuse me of trying to 'adapt Japanese forms'...I admit [being influenced] but claim to have digested it."[127] As for the sometime resemblance between Japanese buildings and his own, it was simply "confirmation" of the universal rightness of the forms that he himself had created—wholly independently.

In 1957, in one of Wright's last repudiations of influence, he emphatically asserted that there was never any outside influence on his architecture.

He did note three exceptions, conceding that he had been influenced by Louis Sullivan, Sullivan's business partner Dankmar Adler and John Roebling, designer of the Brooklyn Bridge.

"My work," Wright went on to say, "is original not only in fact but in spiritual fiber. No practice of any European architect to this day has influenced mine in the least," and as for "the Incas, the Mayans, even the Japanese—all were to me but splendid confirmation [of my own original genius]."[128]

Despite such staunch denials (a small dog with a nasty bark, Wright's protests were outsized), however original one might be, no mind is an island in terms of the mix of contributing ingredients in the creative process.

What distinguished Wright from others was not an immunity from influence. It was instead the ease with which his imaginative powers sought out, realized the potential of and adapted for his purposes the richest, most disparate menu of influences—which, apparently, he could not admit.

To name just a handful of factors, throughout his long, productive life, he embraced and made prolific use of the finest characteristics of his Welsh ancestry, transcendentalism, Unitarianism, Beethoven, Bach, Japonisme, nature, kindergarten, industrialization, the arts and crafts tradition, Louis Sullivan, streamlined automobiles and proto-modern building design.

INDUSTRIAL SURGE

As for the rural community of Mason City, it, too, was never an island. Like Wright, it was inevitably swayed by the widest range of circumstances—from municipal to national to worldwide—in terms of how and when it thrived.

The city's access to the river provided an ample supply of fresh water, a ready convenience of transport and occasions to make industrial use of water power.

The city's first sawmill was constructed on the Winnebago River in 1855, followed in 1870 by a flour mill, called Parker's Mill. Located on Willow Creek, adjacent to land that would later become Rock Crest/Rock Glen, the latter's big stone wheel could make eighty barrels of wheat flour per day.[129]

Soon, a second mill sprang up, and the success of these and other enterprises, spurred by the arrival of five railroad lines, enabled a boom in industrial growth. Soon, there was a lumber yard, a physician, a post office, a grocery store, a blacksmith shop, barbershops, a newspaper, a public library, a photographer, lawyers, banks and bankers, a movie theater, opera houses, churches and schools. In 1870, the population of Mason City was 1,183. Ten years later, it had more than doubled to 2,510, and by 1920, it had reached the then phenomenal total of more than 20,000.[130] As the city's population swelled, the need for building construction increased. While trees were sometimes plentiful in areas next to the rivers, they were typically in short supply on the open prairies. High-quality, durable lumber, required for lasting construction, usually had to be shipped in.

The prospects for building construction improved in the last quarter of the nineteenth century, when it was determined that, west and south of Mason City, there were massive underground reserves of blue and yellow clay, sometimes as deep as forty feet.

This resource was a godsend, since the clay was ideally suited for the manufacture of bricks for building construction, for making cement and for producing drainage tiles that farmers so desperately needed to ensure reliable yields from their crops.

By 1882, a single Mason City firm was producing 400,000 bricks per year. Ten years later saw the founding of the Mason City Brick and Tile Company, followed not long after by a multitude of other plants, especially those for brick and tile.

By 1912, the year when actual construction began on the Rock Crest/Rock Glen neighborhood, Mason City was manufacturing "more brick and tile and more Portland Cement than any city of any size in the world."[131]

The eventual role that the city would play in the cement industry was contingent on the presence of large deposits of limestone (like those that form the limestone bluffs in the Rock Crest/Rock Glen vicinity).

Clay and limestone can be mixed to make a material called Portland cement. Developed in the early nineteenth century and refined by mid-century, it was referred to as "Portland" simply because its initial white-gray color resembled that of Portland stone, a limestone that is quarried on the Isle of Portland, in Dorset, England.

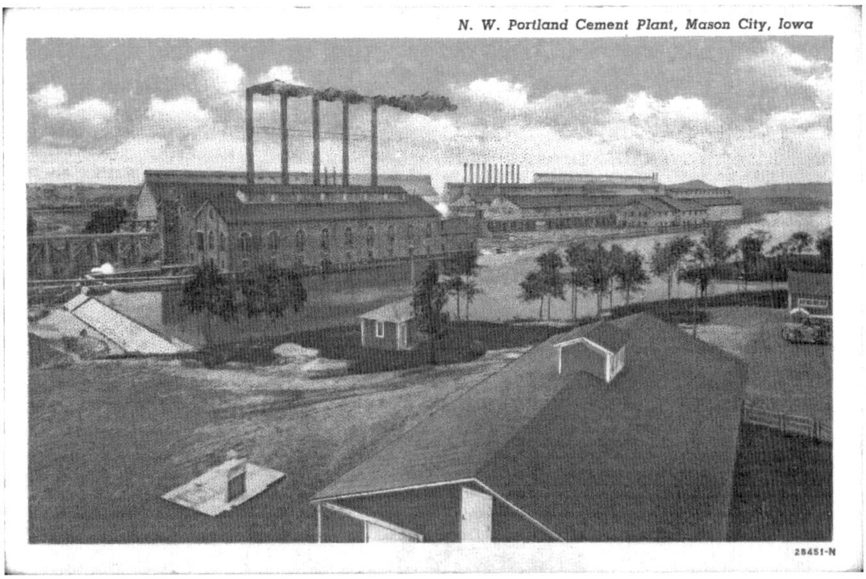

Vintage postcard of the Northwestern States Portland Cement Company in Mason City. *Author's collection.*

A Fireproof House for $5000

Estimated to Cost That Amount in Chicago, and Designed Especially for The Journal

By Frank Lloyd Wright

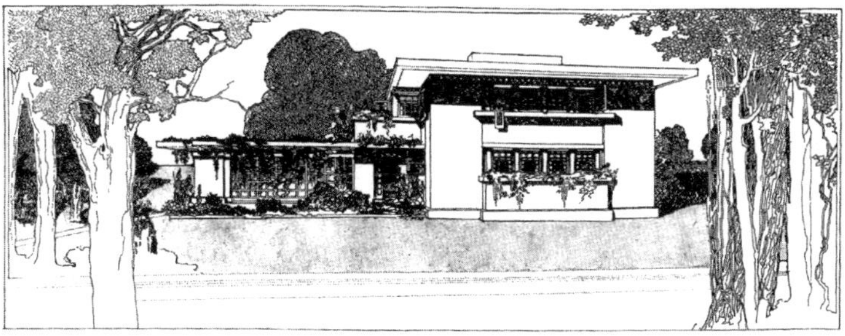

Advertisement for Wright's concrete fireproof house in a 1907 issue of the *Ladies' Home Journal*.

By 1908, Mason City had become the location of the Northwestern States Portland Cement Company, whose success soon after brought to town a branch of a competing firm, the Lehigh Portland Cement Company of Pennsylvania.[132]

The prominence of Mason City in relation to the production of Portland cement is of additional interest because Frank Lloyd Wright was an early contributor to its use in building construction.[133]

As early as 1901, he had designed a pavilion for the Universal Portland Cement Company at the Pan-American Exposition in Buffalo. Nine years later, in December 1910, soon after returning from Europe, his first public commission was a pavilion exhibition in New York for the Cement Show, an event that hoped to demonstrate the advantages of building houses with concrete.[134]

Such houses were, for one thing, fireproof—a virtue Wright had emphasized in the house plan he had published in the *Ladies' Home Journal*. It was also resistant to dampness, and as Wright's later buildings showed, the range of shapes it could take on were all but unlimited. Concrete was also less costly than certain other materials, as Wright had proven earlier in his 1907 design for the Unity Temple in Oak Park.

Agricultural Growth

When agriculture is mentioned, among the things that come to mind are animals raised for consumption, such as cattle, hogs, sheep and chickens. Consistent with that, in the history of Mason City, a leading industrial component became what is euphemistically called "meatpacking." It includes the rote and unpleasant procedures by which farm animals are slaughtered, processed, cleaned and packaged for distribution as food, along with a wide range of byproducts.[135]

Assembly line slaughterhouses (mainly for hogs and cattle) had flourished in Cincinnati (known then as Porkopolis) since the early nineteenth century and rapidly spread to Chicago. Henry Ford supposedly said that the automobile "assembly" line occurred to him by watching the step-by-step killing and "dis-assembly" of hogs in a pork-producing plant.

Meatpacking was made especially viable by the profusion of railroad lines, as well as by provisions for refrigerated storage and transportation. The first meatpacking plant in Mason City was established in the mid-1890s. Subsequently purchased by Jacob Decker, its yearly production soon increased to ten times what it had been before.[136] In 1930, it was purchased by Chicago's Armour Packing Company and became the largest source of jobs in Mason City.

Other agricultural products that come to mind are the area's major farm crops, such as corn, soybeans, hay and oats. In addition, it may be surprising to learn that, for many years, Mason City was an industrial hub for the production of beet sugar, a crop that grew out of a curious past.

In the United States, beet sugar was initially made by New England abolitionists (some of whom were no doubt transcendentalists), who campaigned to boycott the use of West Indies cane sugar, which was harvested by slaves.

In 1917, the Northern Beet Sugar Company established a major processing plant in Mason City, a facility described back then as "one of the most efficient beet sugar factories in the world."[137]

The city was chosen, the article said, because it is

> *in the heart of one of the finest agricultural sections of the country. It has five railroads leading into it, thus affording ample transportation facilities for the movement of beets from the surrounding growing districts to the factory and for the distribution of the high grade granulated sugar which the factory will produce.*[138]

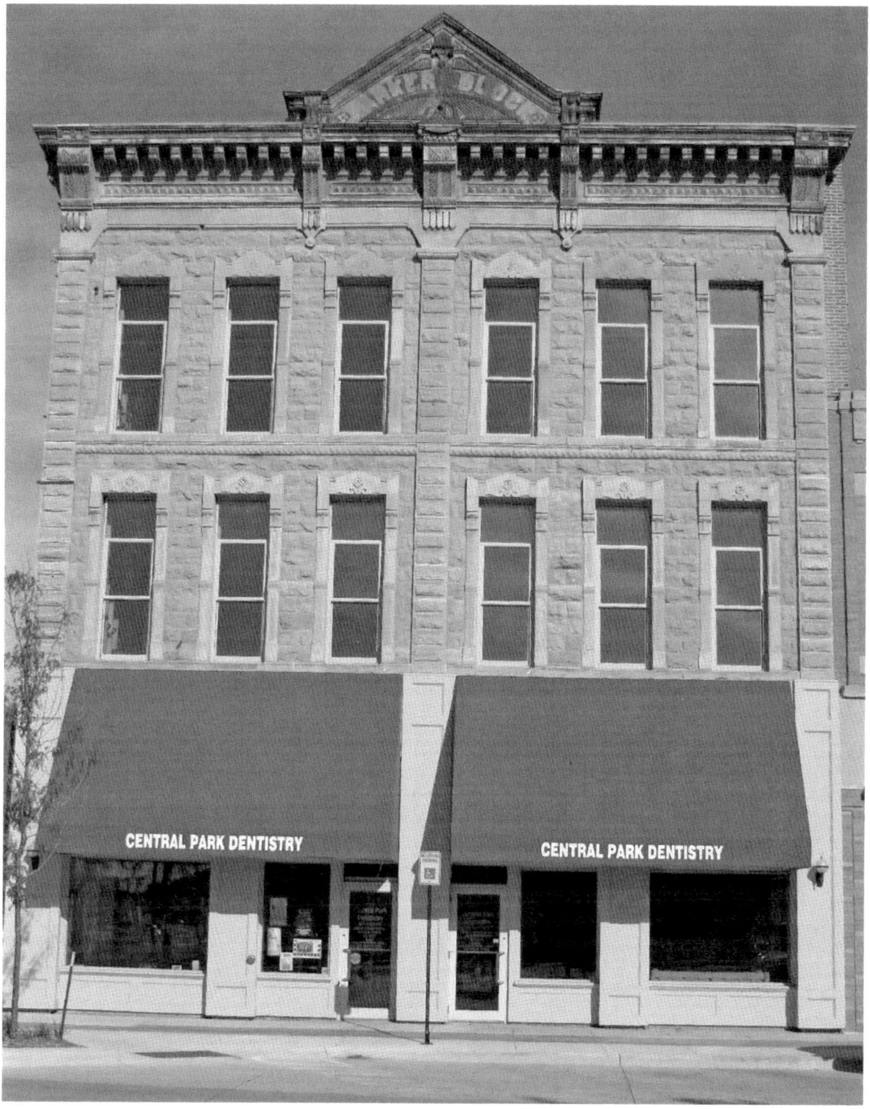

Industrialization brought low-paying employment for Mason City workers, but it also brought cultural amenities, such as the Parker Opera House. *Photograph by Dan Breyfogle (Wikimedia Commons).*

Another advantage, the article adds, is that "a large supply of limestone is on the site, thus eliminating the need of importing this most essential material for sugar production," not to mention the virtue of having "an abundance of pure water."

Among the company's personnel was a chemist named William M. Baird (the father of puppeteer and entertainer Bil Baird, who grew up in Mason City), who was described when he died in 1933 as "the man who designed and built the Mason City sugar factory and who for 40 years was a prominent figure in the beet sugar industry in the middle west."[139]

The steady increase in local employment opportunities, the bulk of which were low-paying and sometimes hazardous jobs, attracted a flood of newcomers. In the years between 1910 and 1926, according to Robert McCoy, "Mason City had the highest growth rate [of any city] in Iowa and the third highest proportion of 'new immigrants' in the state."[140] Of the newest arrivals in those years, a significant number were of Greek origin, as well as Eastern Europeans, thus enriching the cultural fabric.

Beyond the reach of the city itself, what had once been tall-grass prairie increasingly became transformed into vast stretches of cultivated farmland—and more so today than ever before. As one century was shape-shifting seamlessly into the next, industrialization had taken command, and modern design had come with it.[141]

In the years that led up to World War I—which tragically could be described as industrialization applied to the slaughter of our own species—a fortuitous set of conditions prevailed that prompted a once-remote region (a "microcosm of America's industrial and westward expansion," to quote McCoy) to decide to construct, to underwrite financially and to savor the cultural benefits of a radically new architectural style—Prairie School—a style that mirrored the city's surroundings.[142]

3

CITY NATIONAL BANK AND PARK INN HOTEL

In 1911, in an editorial in the November issue of the *Western Architect*, negative observations were made about Frank Lloyd Wright as a residential architect. The article referred to one of his house designs as "practically a freak," then added that no other architect has "failed so signally in the production of livable houses."[143]

For unknown reasons (maybe a stream of subscribers' complaints), the magazine's very next issue made an odd turnabout. Instead of denouncing Wright's architecture, its opening article was a five-page feature about one of his recent building projects, located in Mason City, Iowa—albeit a bank, not a livable house.[144]

Wright's Bank and Hotel

The project played up in the magazine was, of course, the City National Bank and Park Inn Hotel. As eight photographs in the article show (although the text dwells almost exclusively on the bank), it was essentially two buildings whose functions far exceeded those of a bank and a hotel.

The tandem City National Bank and Park Inn would in time be lauded as a pivotal achievement in Wright's career. He designed only six hotels in his life (only five of those were actually built), all of which were created between 1908 and 1923, the Park Inn being the second and the only one that still survives.

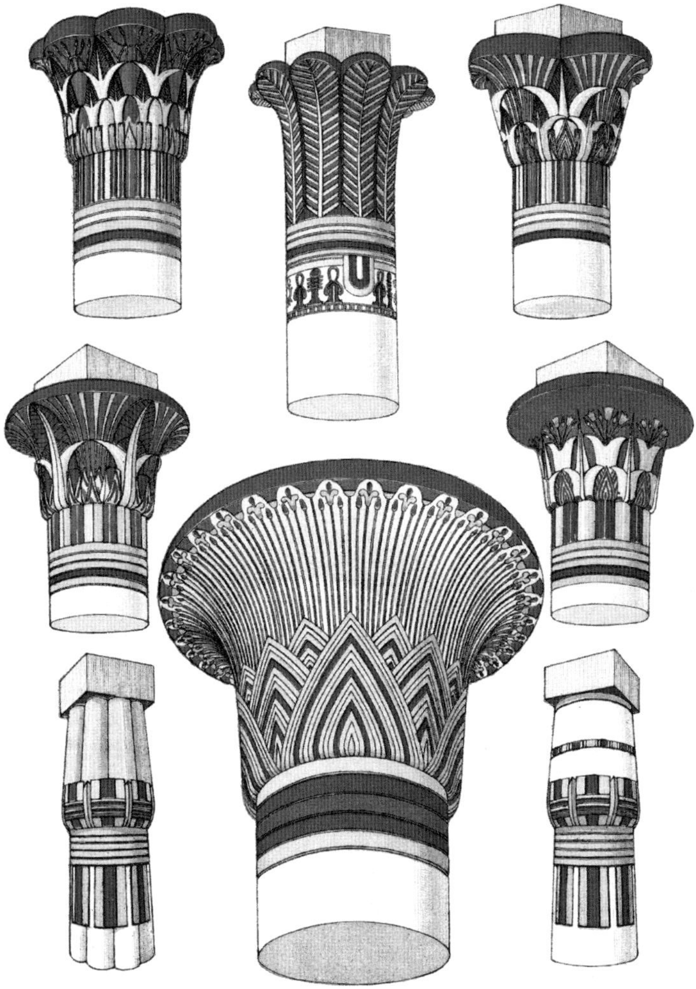

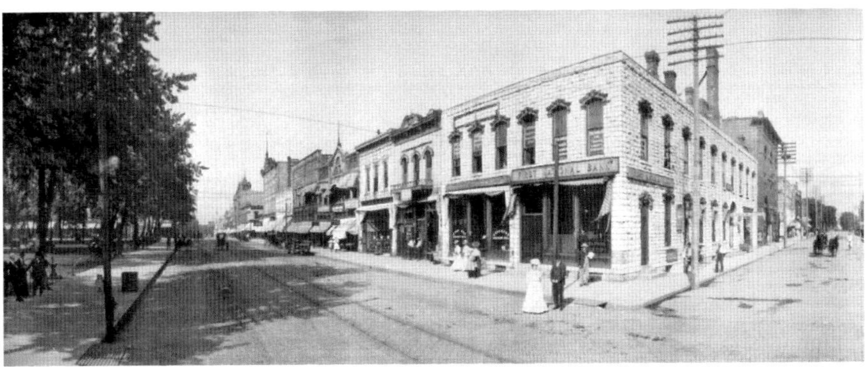

Structurally, Wright designed the two buildings to function as non-identical twins, distinct yet inseparable entities that are linked by a shared transitional zone, a generic first-floor entrance that is now known as the "central waist."

The buildings were commissioned by the board of directors of the long-established City National Bank, which had been founded initially in 1884 as the City Bank. The original Italianate building for that facility (still standing and itself restored, it is now a clothing store) was located at 1 South Main Street, directly east and across the street from the eventual location of the new bank building of the same name.[145]

In order to plan the new building, Wright traveled to Mason City, most likely by train, from Chicago. No one seems to know for sure how many times he visited, but one news story at the time claims that he was "frequently" in town. According to another source, when he did visit, he stayed at the Markley home.[146]

These visits apparently happened in 1907–08, at which time he studied the bank's proposed construction site, which could easily be observed from the intersection of the two major downtown streets, Main Street (renamed Federal Avenue in 1916), a major north–south city street that cuts through the business center, and State Street, which spans the city east–west. At the time of Wright's visits, Main Street was the city's busiest thoroughfare. By

Opposite, top: Lithographic plate from *The Grammar of Ornament* (1856) by Owen Jones, an indispensable sourcebook for architects.

Opposite, bottom: Left half of a panoramic photograph of downtown Mason City in 1907. Photograph by Frederick J. Bandholtz. *LOC Prints and Photographs*.

Below: Right half of the same panoramic photograph, looking south on Main Street. Photograph by Frederick J. Bandholtz. *LOC Prints and Photographs*.

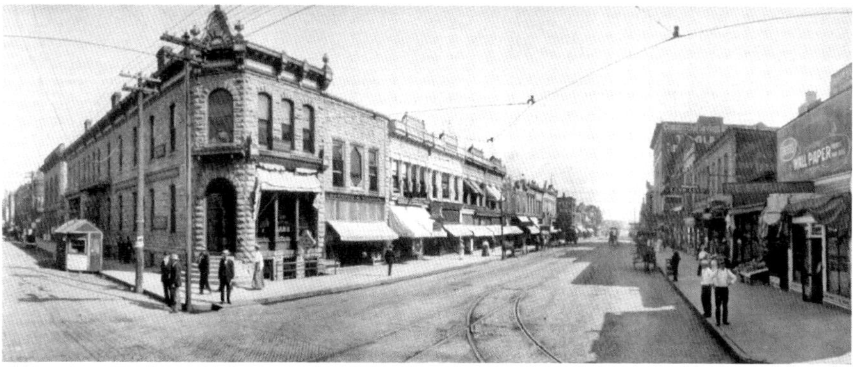

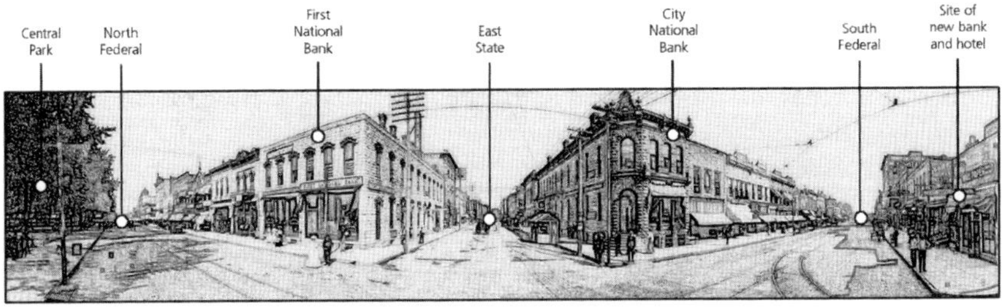

Digital drawing of the same view of Mason City in 1907, as photographed at the intersection of Main Street (Federal) and State. *Author's diagram.*

comparison, State Street was less congested, quieter and more subdued, in part because it is the edge of a square-block public park.

All of this was substantially changed as recently as 1985, when, in the hope of revitalization, several north–south blocks were closed and replaced by a downtown shopping mall. The traffic route that had formerly been Federal Avenue was split and then diverted to separate parallel byways, named Washington and Delaware Avenues. Those two-pronged one-way streets now serve as Highway 65.

Central Park

Set aside for community use in 1855, the city's so-called Central Park was (and is) a refuge for park bench relaxation, a convenient location for public events, as well as a place to reflect on aspects of the city's past.[147]

The park's most conspicuous feature then (and to a lesser extent today) is a tall monument, erected in 1883, in memory of Cerro Gordo County citizens who perished in the Civil War. It is also a fitting reminder that no other state in the Union, proportionate to its population, contributed more soldiers to that devastating conflict than did Iowa. Nearly half of all males in Iowa served in the Civil War; thirteen thousand of them died in battle, from disease, in POW camps or due to other circumstances.[148]

If Mason City's Central Park is at all familiar, it may be for good reason. This same Iowa community was the boyhood home of American composer and playwright Meredith Willson.

Willson was the author of several well-known Broadway musicals, of which the most unforgettable is *The Music Man*, which was later made into a popular film. The setting for the story is a fictional Iowa community called River City, aspects of which were heavily based on Willson's childhood experiences in Mason City.[149]

As a result, in the community's tourist promotions, the name Mason City is used interchangeably with its Broadway (and Hollywood) nickname: River City.

In a poignant moment in Willson's film, the main character (a music professor and con man named Harold Hill) speaks to a gathering of gullible townspeople at the base of a statue in a tranquil public park. "Yuh got trouble," Hill warns the city's impressionable citizens, "right here in River City."[150] The park in the film is a caricature of Mason City's Central Park.

Each year, Mason City celebrates the achievements of Willson, the city's undisputed favorite son. The composer's birthplace is a house museum on South Pennsylvania Avenue, where it stands beside a multimedia complex for tourists called Music Man Square, which includes a movie set streetscape of the musical's mythical city, the Meredith Willson Museum, a banquet center and various music-themed facilities.[151]

Aside from Meredith Willson's celebrity, and the city's increasing distinction as a historic architectural site, its other well-known claim to fame is its proximity to the Surf Ballroom (west of the city in Clear Lake) and the Mason City airport, where rock-and-roll musicians Buddy Holly, Ritchie Valens and J.P. (the Big Bopper) Richardson perished in an airplane crash in 1959.[152]

Other accomplished Americans were born, grew up, resided or died in Mason City. Among them were puppeteer Bil Baird, who created the marionettes for the film version of *The Sound of Music*; Merle Armitage, a celebrated book designer, art director and theater impresario, mentioned earlier; Carrie Chapman Catt, a famous women's suffrage advocate; and U.S. Army general Hanford (Jack) MacNider, assistant secretary of war and ambassador to Canada.

General MacNider was the son of Mason City businessman Charles H. MacNider, for whom the city's MacNider Art Museum is named and who successfully took over management of the Northwestern States Portland Cement Company, the lucrative building materials firm that was founded by his father.[153]

Charles H. MacNider was also a prominent banker who built a large, six-story structure for the First National Bank in 1910 (in part as a business rivalry with the City National Bank), replacing its earlier building. MacNider's bank would soon become the largest in the state.

MacNider was a powerful, well-connected political foe of the directors of the City National Bank, and the construction of his new high-rise bank was timed in part to coincide with the completion of the three-story building that Wright had been commissioned to build. MacNider's new First National Bank was at that same intersection of Federal and State, facing the park, cater-corner across the street from its then competitor.[154]

A colorful, if now mostly amusing, event in Mason City history was the robbery of the First National Bank on March 13, 1934, by gangsters John Dillinger, Baby Face Nelson and five others, who were equipped with Thompson submachine guns (referred to then as "Tommy guns").

The Mason City police, armed only with .38-caliber handguns (and certainly not amused at the time), watched helplessly from sheltered posts behind large rocks in downtown Central Park. The bank robbers scored $52,000 that afternoon, before successfully speeding away with a carload of hostages.[155]

Mediating Differences

As for the City National Bank and Park Inn, it was a formidable challenge for Wright to design a three-story building in which the primary functions were both those of a bank and a hotel. And if that were not enough, he was also required to include additional suitable spaces for a law firm (Blythe, Markley, Rule and Smith), rental spaces and retail shops.

In the end, Wright's way of addressing the problem was at once shrewd and resourceful. He positioned the bank in such a way that its imposing, fortress-like entrance opened onto Main Street (now Federal Avenue), where high-powered business exchanges took place. In contrast, the front entrance of the hotel bordered on State Street, where it faced the tranquil downtown park. As a result, the City National Bank and Main Street were mutually suitable in temperament, as were the Park Inn and Central Park.

There is a muted resemblance between Wright's architectural solution and Friedrich Froebel's second kindergarten gift (the educator's favorite), consisting of a wooden sphere, a cube and a cylinder. As discussed earlier, Froebel had provided a mediation between the two opposing shapes of the sphere and the cube (*thesis* and *antithesis*) by bridging them with the transitional form of the cylinder (*synthesis*), which shares attributes with both.[156] Not surprisingly, Froebel was strongly influenced by German philosopher Georg Wilhelm Friedrich Hegel.

In Wright's design for the combined bank and hotel, he may have thought in a similar way: he placed the bank at one end, facing east, with the Park

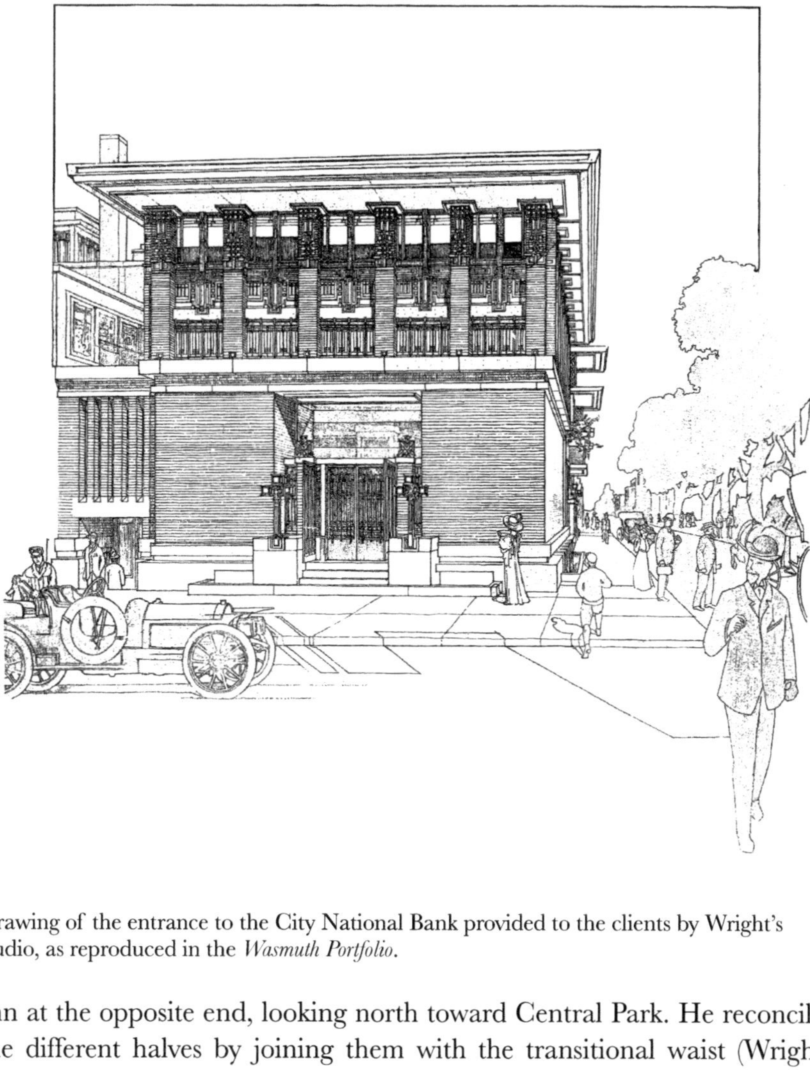

Drawing of the entrance to the City National Bank provided to the clients by Wright's studio, as reproduced in the *Wasmuth Portfolio*.

Inn at the opposite end, looking north toward Central Park. He reconciled the different halves by joining them with the transitional waist (Wright's equivalent to the cylinder), which served to soften the difference between the needs and functions of the bank as distinct from those of the hotel.

The waist, at the same time, was a pragmatically functional feature, since it allowed for separate access to the law firm, rental offices and retail shops. It had been the clients' intention that the entrance to the waist would be the building's primary door to the street.

But of course, there was more to Wright's design than simply that. He also implanted connections between the two buildings by setting up a web of rhymes.

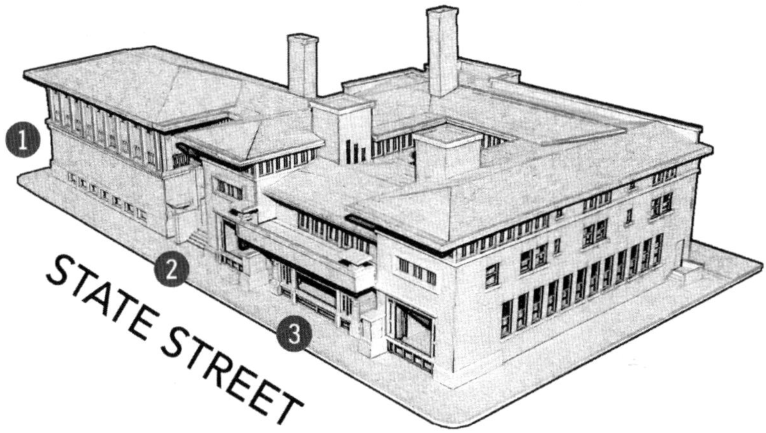

Model of the City National Bank and Park Inn as of 1910. The hotel (1) is in the foreground; the bank entrance (not visible) is at the upper left (1), while the transitional waist is at (2) and the Park Inn entrance is at (3). *Diagram from author's photograph.*

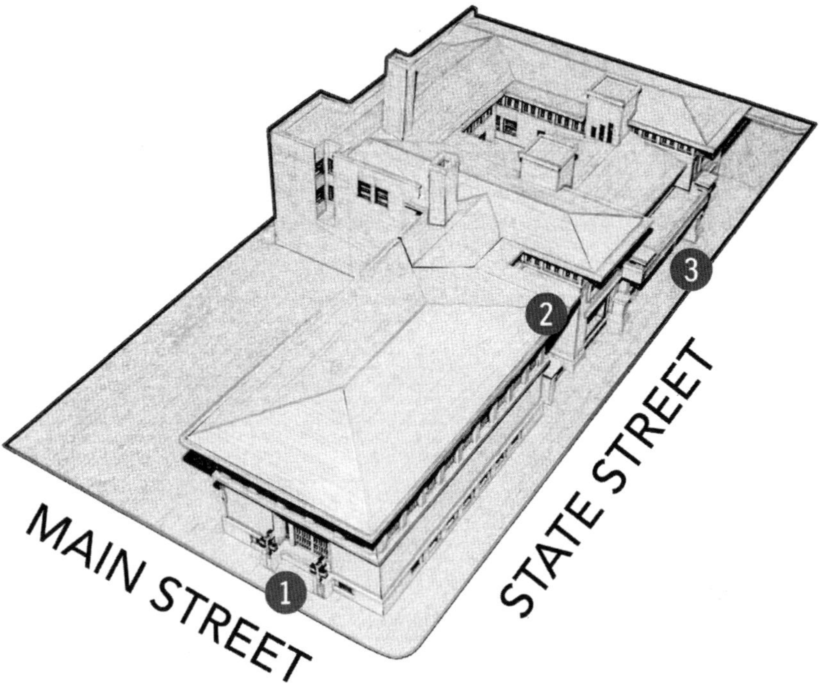

The same model as viewed from the northeast, with the same numbering system. Both renderings are based on a model exhibited at the McCoy Architectural Interpretive Center. *Diagram from author's photograph.*

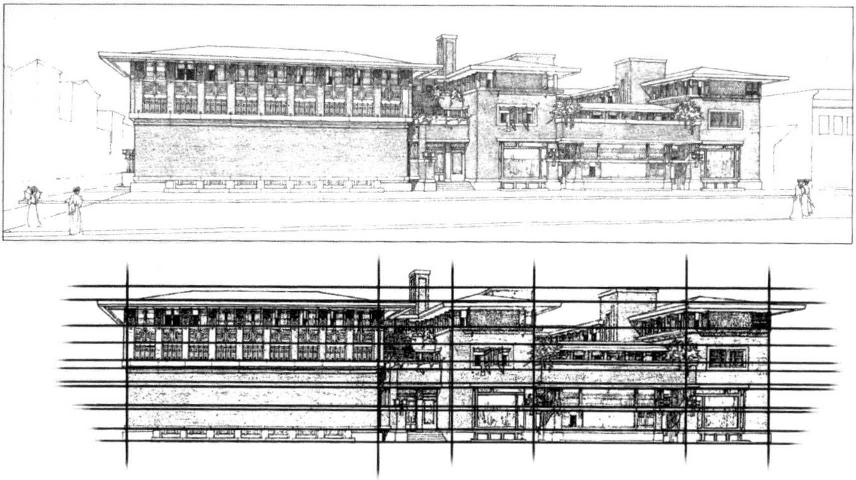

Wright's elevation drawing of the north face of the bank and hotel (from the *Wasmuth Portfolio*) and (below that) a diagram of the buildings' line ideas. *Public domain with author's diagram.*

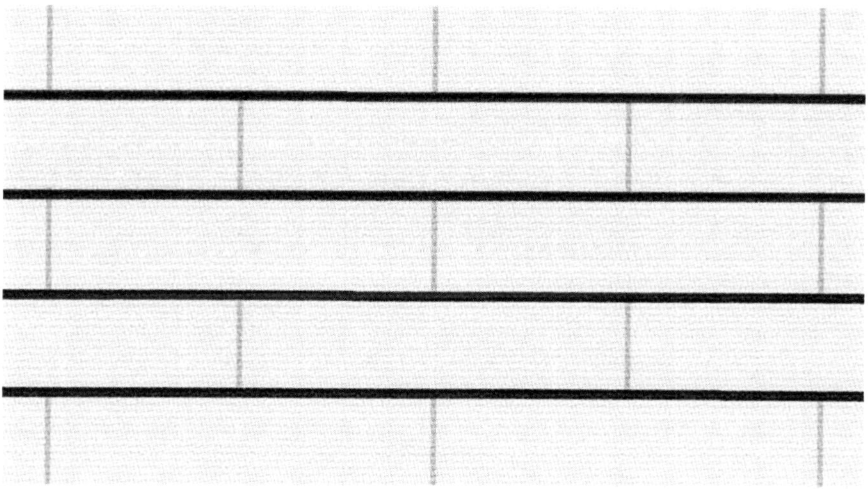

Wright frequently strengthened horizontal lines by using lighter colors of mortar in the vertical gaps between the bricks. *Author's diagram.*

He accomplished this in various ways: by aligning the overhanging roofs; by matching the heights and proportions of various key components; by repeating the widths and thicknesses of horizontal concrete bands; by the continuity of color (including, on the upper floors, colored terra-cotta tiles);

by the selective positioning of abstract art glass windows; and by the repeated use of the same building materials (especially brick, concrete and glass).

Looking closely at a profile of the two buildings from across the street in Central Park, one can imagine how Arthur Wesley Dow might have sketched out the layout scheme (recalling the line ideas he found in Ukiyo-e woodblock prints) that tacitly contributes to the unity of the two buildings while also maintaining the gesture of the outreach of the prairie.

In addition, as he often did in brick buildings, Wright underscored the horizontality of both buildings by the use of what bricklayers call raked horizontal mortar joints combined with flush-pointed vertical joints.[157] He amplified this by using two different colors of mortar, in which the vertical gaps between two bricks are filled with a brick-matching mortar, while the horizontal spaces are filled with a contrasting color of mortar that stands out and supports the illusion of lateral lines.

Large-Scale Strong Box

It turns out that the text in the *Western Architect* article was written by Wright himself. It had been published initially in the *Mason City Times* (November 5, 1910) under the headline "City National Bank Moves to Its New Home." A note that accompanies the article states that it was "prepared for this newspaper by the architect Frank Lloyd Wright."

In the *Western Architect*, the article starts by revealing that the bank's design is based on the assumption that "a bank building is itself a strong box on a large scale; a well aired and lighted fireproof vault."[158]

And indeed, when viewed in profile from the park, the bank component looks unquestionably solid and stable. Its massive walls appear to form an impenetrable stone fortress, with no openings and no access to the outside except through the ominous ceremonial front entrance (both elevated and recessed).

One problem, of course, is that a vault-like box with solid walls does not allow for much lighting. In addition, how can an architect ensure the compatibility of a large-scale strong box with a markedly different topmost floor of inviting, well-lit offices?

In addressing the issue of lighting, Wright made use of a spatial illusion. At the top of the massive expanse of the outside wall, he caps what first appears to be the ceiling of the first floor with a ledge-like horizontal band

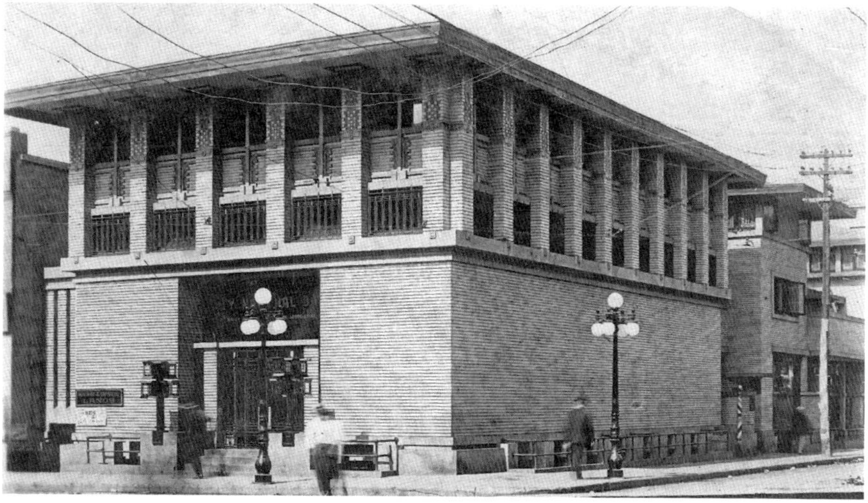

Photograph of the exterior of the City National Bank shortly after its completion (circa 1910). *Mason City Public Library.*

or belt, a feature that strongly echoes a gravity-grounded concrete band at the base of the building's foundation.

What is disarming (as well as delightful) from the outside is that the row of windows that begin at the top of that ledge-like concrete band are not really a second floor at all (it is architectural sleight of hand). Instead, those windows extend the bank's ceiling inside, making the ground floor two stories tall, while the row of windows at the top provide both ventilation and light.

Only above that deceptive ceiling does the floor of the rental offices start, which themselves are cheerfully lighted by a plentiful border of art glass windows. In the article, Wright describes these windows as a "richly varied frieze" that animates the topmost "crown."[159]

Viewed from the street, this creates the impression of a structure of two equal layers. That effect is reinforced in the upper half by a sequence of thirty-two brick pillars—six of which run across the front and rear, with ten each spaced along the sides. Because of those square-shaped pillars (or columns), the top half of the building appears to be just as substantial as the half below.

In the end, the building's bottom portion (the so-called strong box) appears to be reassuringly thick, as one would expect of the walls of a bank, yet the top is conspicuously playful because of its colorful art glass windows and ornate interplay of tiles.

Inside and Out

Understandably (for security reasons, if nothing else) there is not a profusion of photographs of the bank's interior. The architect's floor plans have survived (there are at least two different versions), but there are few other records of the bank interior that predate 1926.

Among the surviving photographs (not reproduced here) are those that Wright included in his 1911 article in the *Western Architect*.[160] These show the bank's interior as if the viewer had stepped inside. The horizontal brick motif that is on the exterior walls is continued on the inside. In the center, there is a gated customer service zone that bears the same design treatment, with three bank teller windows.[161]

There are also photographs of the bank's ornate, imposing vault. It is in the center, behind the tellers' island, in a separate fireproof, brick-lined room. Its arched entrance wall looks like the hearth in a Wrightian home.

The board of directors' conference room is lit by art glass windows and skylights and is furnished with Wright-designed table and chairs.[162] In several photographs, the row of clerestory windows above (some of which are open to allow for ventilation) are clearly visible at the intersection of the walls and ceiling.

Mounted on upright posts that overlook the tellers' space are four ornate lighting fixtures. They are identical figurative sculptures of the *Spirit of Mercury* ("the patron of commerce and finance," according to Wright) in a form created by Richard Bock, a German-born American artist who was frequently commissioned by architects (including Wright, repeatedly) to create site-specific art.[163]

There are also decorative references to the abstract terra-cotta designs that are on the exterior second floor, as well as smaller versions of a typically Prairie School concrete urn that occurs in larger versions on the exterior second floor, above the hotel entrance and, on street level, at the door of the transitional waist.[164]

Unlike the interior of the bank, the alterations to its exterior are reasonably well documented, mostly because of its easy access. There are quite a few news photographs, amateur snapshots and vintage postcards (some colorized) that document the changes (as well as stages of neglect) to the building's exterior from year to year. To make a long story short, it was ravaged architecturally. The interior was demolished, and the outside all but died as well.[165]

In fact, the bank as Wright designed it survived for less than twenty years. Beginning about 1920, the community (like those in other farming states) was crippled by various economic crises, largely farm-related. Having declared bankruptcy, the City National Bank was forced to close, along with other Mason City banks (at one time there had been as many as five), with the sole exception of the City National's longtime competitor, the First National Bank.

During the 1920s, Iowa led the nation in bank failures. To get a clear sense of the crisis, it is helpful to remember (as described by Leland Sage) that in 1920, the number of bank failures "jumped to 167 and in 1921 shot up to 505, then fell back to 366 in 1922. All through the remaining 1920s the number hovered well above the 500 mark each year."[166]

Transformation and Decline

Soon after, when the foreclosed City National Bank and Park Inn changed ownership in 1926, the new owners (in the hope of financial survival, even revitalization perhaps) decided to convert the bank to walk-in retail stores and office space. In a massive remodeling effort, the bank's interior was gutted. Its first floor was lowered to grade level, and the once spectacular two-story banking room became two normal floors of standard height. Now, there really were three floors.

On the exterior, the most shocking transformation was the conversion of the bank's impenetrable walls to glassed-in commercial storefronts. Thankfully, perhaps for expediency, the least exterior damage was done to the upper level, where the topmost original windows were spared, as were the terra-cotta tiles. For many years afterward, those who knew the building's historical past had only that colorful upper crown to look up at admiringly as they passed the building's sad remains.[167]

Under new ownership, the bank and hotel were divided by an interior wall to enable their potential sale as two distinct properties. Thereafter, at least architecturally, it may be accurate to say that the hotel survived better than the bank, although it, too, was modified. At the very least, it remained a hotel (albeit in disrepair and half empty at times) until 1972, when, after repeated foreclosures, it was unsuccessfully changed into an apartment complex.[168]

When the Park Inn initially opened in 1910, it had been advertised as "European" because it hoped to emulate the exotic charm and ambiance of overseas bed-and-breakfast hotels. The Park Inn and its rooms were small. There was hot and cold water in every room, but as with most hotels back

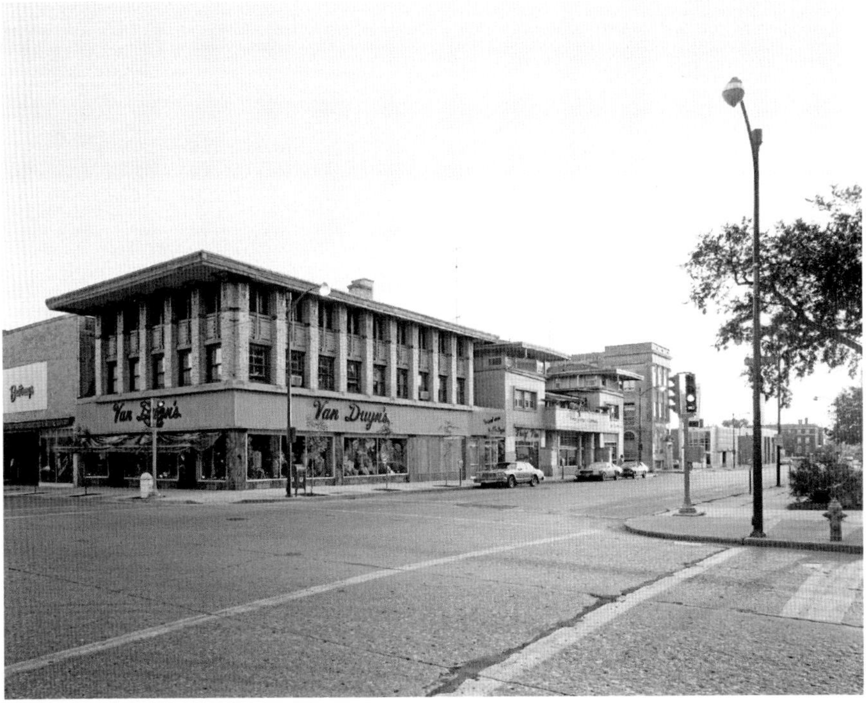
Van Duyn's

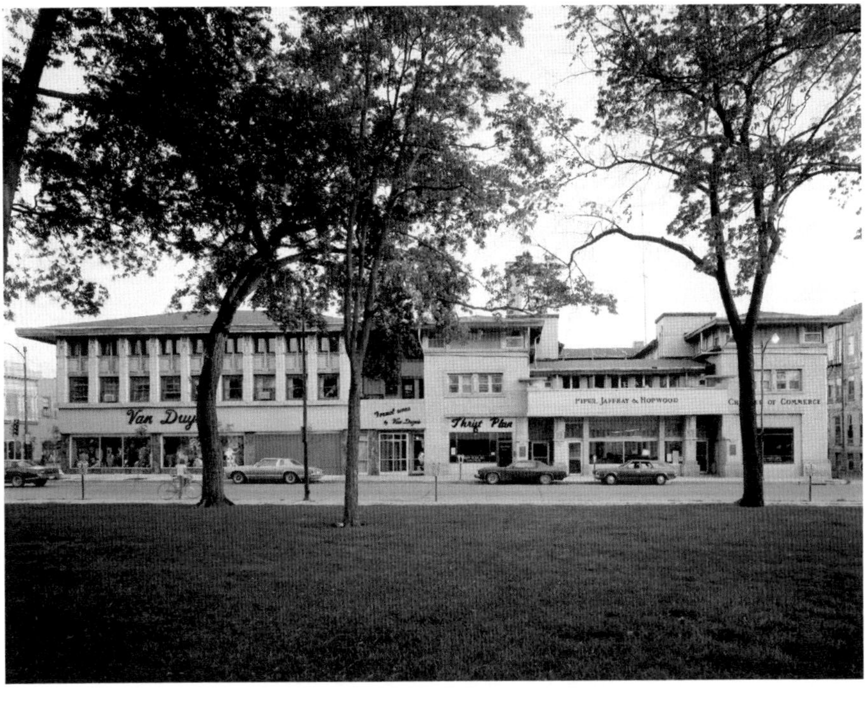
Thrift Plan
PIPER, JAFFRAY & HOPWOOD

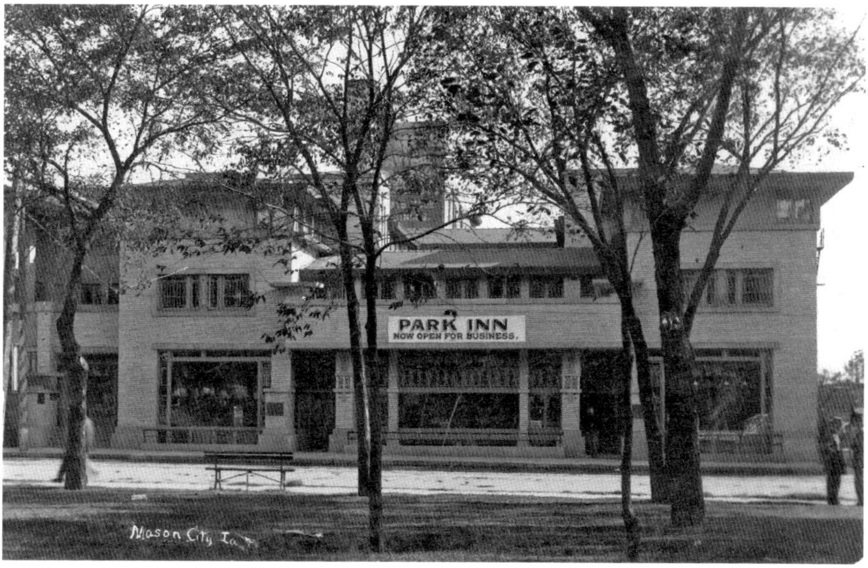

Vintage postcard of the Park Inn Hotel entrance, as viewed from the park (date uncertain). *Mason City Public Library.*

Opposite: The bank and hotel in 1977, clearly showing the ground floor walls that had become glassed-in storefronts. *Historic American Buildings Survey, LOC Prints and Photographs.*

then (except the most expensive), two adjoining rooms shared a bathroom or there was a bathroom off the hall.

In 1910, the hotel publicity claimed it was a model of "cuisine and comfort." It was, the ad continued,

> *a marvelously well planned hostelry, every room of* [its] *sixty-one rooms but one* [in truth, there were only forty guest rooms] *being an outside room with art glass French windows, mahogany furniture, Cadillac tables, brass beds with box mattresses, lavatories with hot and cold water, luxurious bath rooms—everything new and sanitary and comfort wooing.*[169]

The dining area, as the *Mason City Globe Gazette* confirmed, "serves only the 'finest cuisine with a European flair.'"

The Park Inn Hotel was reasonably successful for a dozen years after it opened. Unfortunately, despite the initial send-off and the praise that followed, it had begun to decline irreversibly by 1922.

That year (in the midst of a catastrophic farm crisis) marked the opening of a new downtown hotel, just three blocks from the Park Inn. It was named

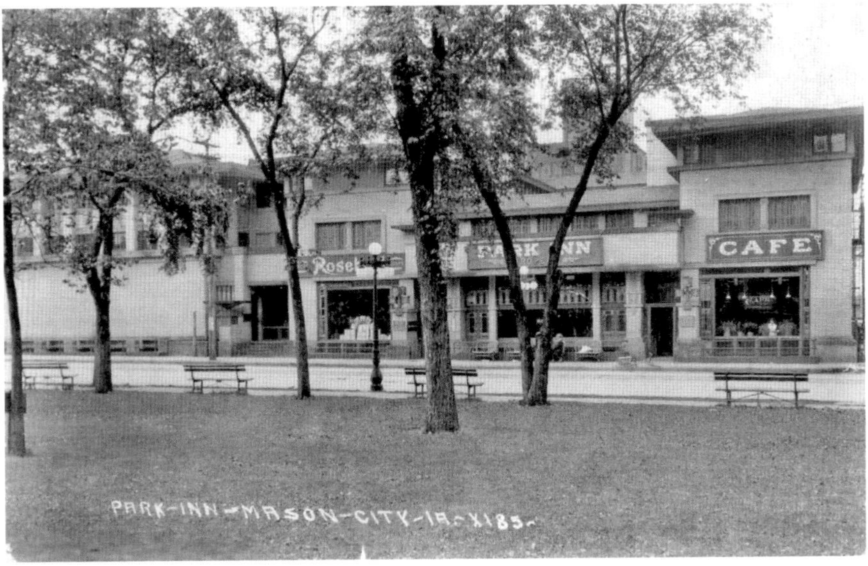

Vintage postcard of the Park Inn Hotel entrance (circa 1920). *Mason City Public Library.*

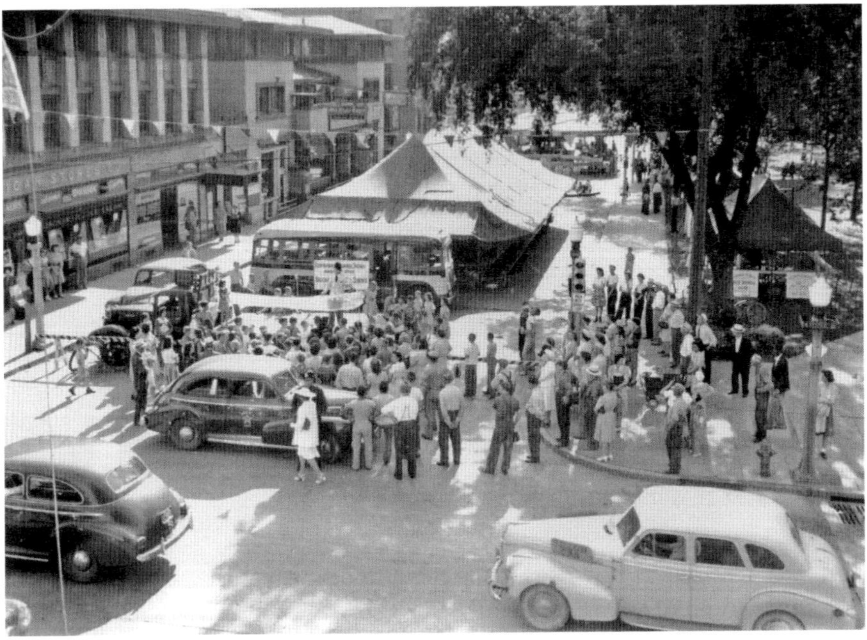

Photograph of a street carnival on State Street in 1943, in front of the City National Bank and Park Inn, which underwent remodeling in 1926. *Mason City Public Library.*

Hotel Hanford, in honor of the family of the wife of Charles H. MacNider, the Mason City banker whose First National Bank had been the long-term competitor of the City National Bank.[170]

The new, much larger hotel was undeniably upscale. Its 250 guest rooms were more spacious and luxurious than those of the Park Inn. In addition, the Park Inn rooms were still limited to shared bathrooms, whereas each Hanford room had its own.

For these and other reasons, the Park Inn's survival was not in the cards. But what looked like an inevitable death would drag on ever so slowly for eight decades or longer.

In 1962, when the film version of Meredith Willson's *The Music Man* premiered in Mason City, the Champagne Supper for the extravaganza was held (of course) at the Hanford Hotel. Among the guests that evening were Hollywood celebrities Robert Preston, Shirley Jones, Ronnie Howard, Arthur Godfrey and Hedda Hopper—all of whom stayed at the Hanford Hotel.

In a 1970 article in the *Des Moines Register* (headlined "Time Cruel to Iowa Hotel by Frank Lloyd Wright"), the Park Inn Hotel's bar and dance floor were described as "not an inviting place."[171]

Pigeons had moved into secluded areas of the building. The roof was leaking, and mold was an ever-present concern. "By 1970," as described by Katherine Haun, "Mason City residents told visitors: 'Don't stay there.'"[172]

All this was taking place just as there was a growing concern about the nation's attitude toward the preservation of historic architecture. Four years earlier, the National Register of Historic Places had been created by the federal government so that communities could seek grant support for the faithful restoration of historic buildings of significance.

Among events that signaled hope for the survival of Wright's bank and hotel were the efforts of a committee of Mason City citizens, who, in 1972, successfully applied to have the bank and hotel listed on the National Register of Historic Places.

Wright's Achievement

In 1997, architectural historian Robert McCarter described Mason City's City National Bank and Park Inn as "a masterpiece of integration."[173]

It is, he went on to say, "one of Wright's most interesting designs of the period, though it is rarely studied." Its integrative richness comes from the

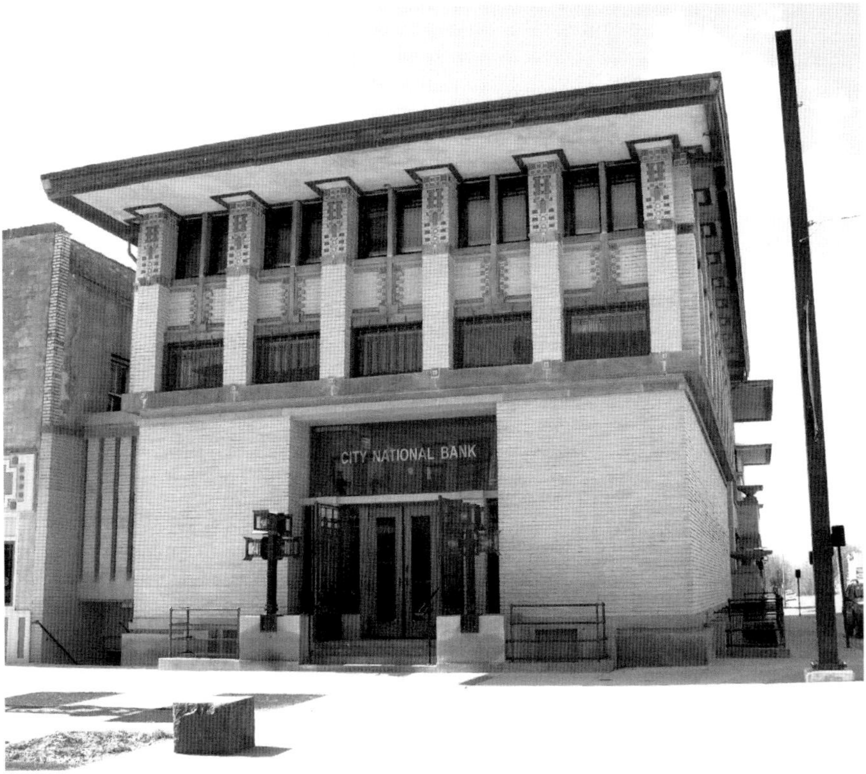

Current exterior view of the City National Bank, as restored in 2011. In the end, the cost of the project was more than $18 million. *Author's photograph.*

back-and-forth dance of connections between the two buildings. Through "complementary massing and fenestration," McCarter concludes, "Wright brings the disparate functional elements into a highly resolved and beautifully proportioned composition."[174]

Despite Wright's achievement, it would not be an easy task to preserve the bank and hotel, much less to restore them to the condition that he had initially planned. As Haun documents, an impassioned exchange of opinions ensued. It went on for years (and still goes on to some extent). Genuine restoration of the building(s) would require an enormous commitment of funds. Funding sources are limited, and the collection and distribution of funds necessitates painful decisions about what is of foremost importance in life—in this case, the life of a city.

Besides, what could possibly be achieved? As was asked in 1989 in the *Mason City Globe Gazette*, in an editorial on the fate of the bank and the hotel,

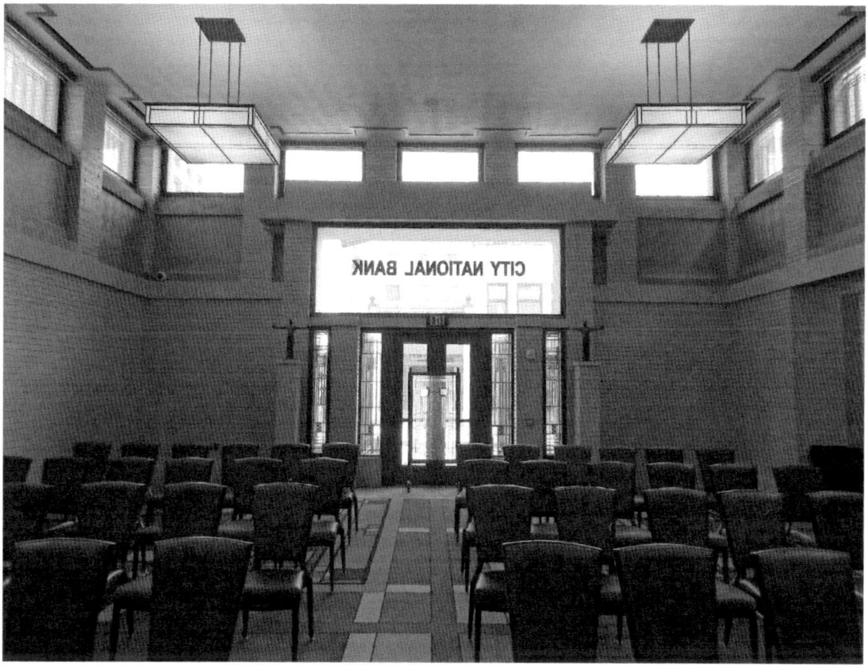

Current interior view of Wright's City National Bank, which now functions as an events facility. *Photograph by Daniel Hartwig (Creative Commons).*

"What function can support that form?" No investors could ever recover their funds. And the city could never afford to restore and then maintain it. Without private funding, the editorial continucd, thc building(s) will continue to be "a crumbling anachronism at worst; at best a lifeless museum memorializing a man who left his mark on the city 79 years ago."[175]

That editorial was written twenty-five years ago. Since then, a miracle has evolved. In truth, it was not really a miracle but the consequence of efforts by Mason City citizens (as well as others from outside) that began as early as 2000 and finally reached a crescendo in 2011. Among those citizens were several who were owners (and protectors) of homes of equal significance in the Rock Crest/Rock Glen neighborhood.

The rescue of Wright's Mason City buildings is a long and meandering story, the details of which have been documented in various publications, available to visitors at the city's McCoy Architectural Interpretive Center, as well as at the gift shop of the Wright on the Park Headquarters. Suffice it to say that, through phenomenal achievements in historical research, fundraising, cooperation and consent, the buildings that had formerly been

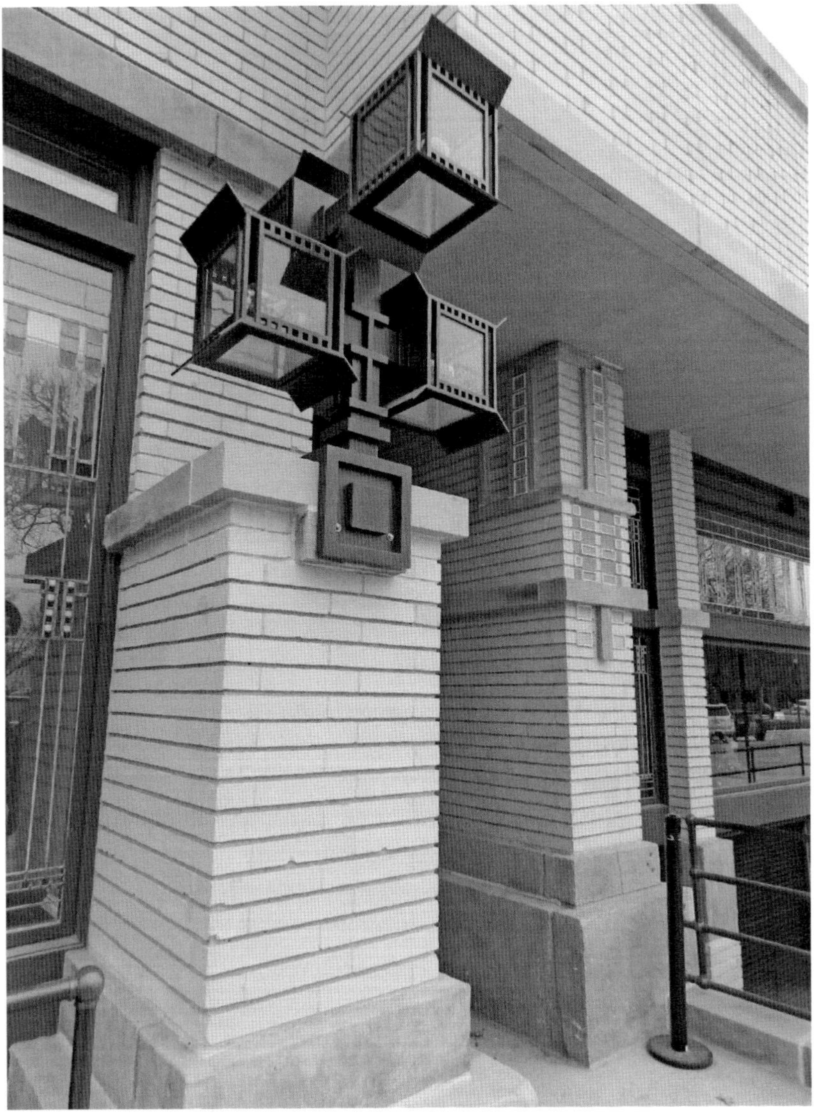

Detail of a current view of Wright's Historic Park Inn Hotel. *Photograph by Daniel Hartwig (Creative Commons).*

the City National Bank and Park Inn were restored and opened once again in 2011 as the Historic Park Inn Hotel.

How fortunate are we today to be able to witness directly—in a visceral and immediate way—a breathtaking triumph in building design that reaffirms human achievement.

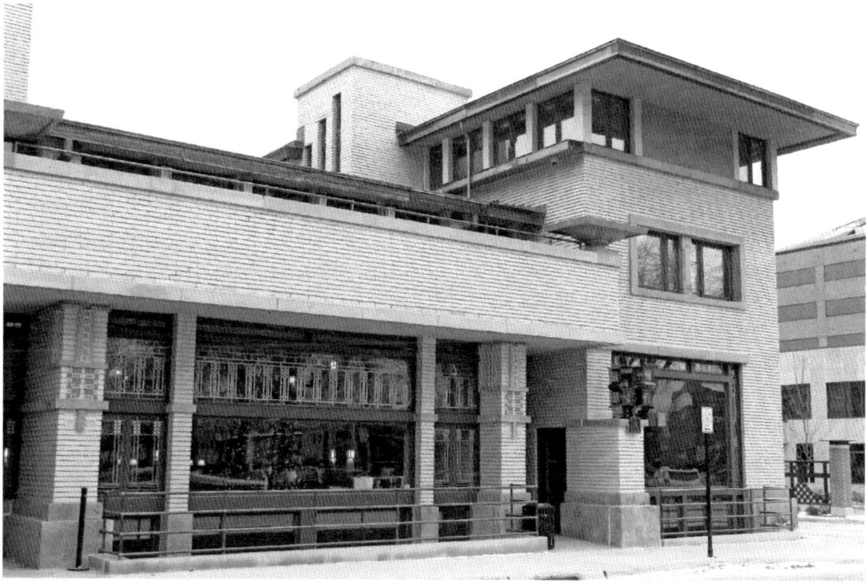

Entrance to the Historic Park Inn Hotel after restoration. Today, it functions prominently as a hotel, restaurant and events facility. *Photograph by Daniel Hartwig (Creative Commons).*

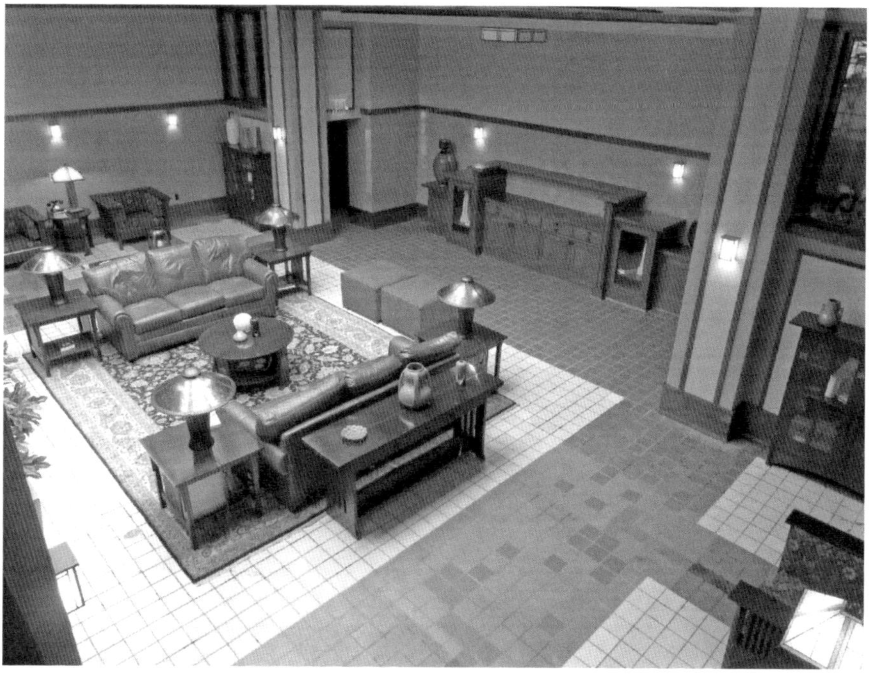

The Skylight Room in the restored Historic Park Inn Hotel interior. *Photograph by Bobak Ha'Eri (Wikimedia Commons).*

In its inspiring restored state, the Historic Park Inn Hotel now thrives as a cultural icon that functions year round as a hotel, restaurant and events facility, where guests (some of whom have traveled here from other countries) can once again experience "bed-and-breakfast" in the setting of an architectural masterpiece.[176]

4

ROCK CREST/ ROCK GLEN NEIGHBORHOOD

In 1903, a Mason City building contractor and real estate developer named Joshua G. Melson purchased twenty-two acres of land on the east edge of the city's downtown. The site was within five blocks of the busy intersection of Main Street (later Federal Avenue) and State Street, where, seven years later, the new City National Bank and Park Inn would be erected.

Melson's property was an undeveloped subdivision overlooking Willow Creek, a tributary of Lime Creek, now called the Winnebago River. The terrain on the banks of the river included limestone bluffs on the eastern high ground side, part of which is known today as Rock Crest. On the opposite side of the stream, there was low ground on the western plane, called Rock Glen.[177]

River Heights

Melson subdivided his (the higher) portion of the land, naming it River Heights, and prepared to offer lots for sale. The land on the opposite side of the stream would soon be owned by others, among them the bankers and lawyers who would commission Wright's design of the bank and hotel.

As mentioned earlier, while Wright was working on the City National Bank and Park Inn in 1908, he also designed a Prairie School home for a local doctor and his wife, now known as the Stockman House.

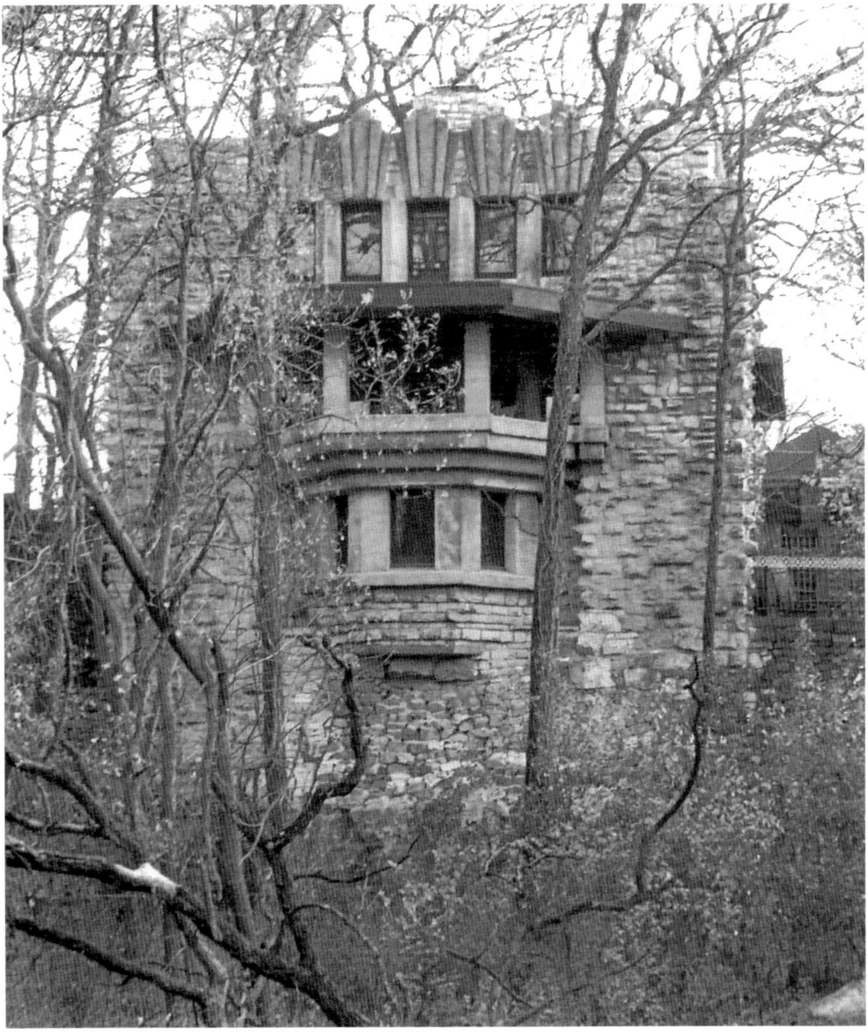

A view of the back of the Melson House in its restored state and the limestone bluff it rests on. *Photograph courtesy Peggy L. Bang ©2015.*

Joshua Melson was a building contractor who had dabbled in house design. While not trained as an architect, he had an insatiable interest in architecture and had worked as an apprentice to another Mason City contractor and self-taught architect, E.R. Bogardus. He admired Wright's proposal for the Stockman House.[178]

From all reports, Melson was unusually open to innovation, architectural and otherwise. He was the owner of one of the first automobiles in Cerro

Gordo County (it was the first electric car in the state), and in 1919, he acquired the area's first passenger airplane, a Canadian wartime Curtiss surplus plane, and he trained as an amateur pilot.[179]

When Melson saw the Stockman House, it occurred to him to talk to Wright about designing a distinctive home for himself (an unusual showcase dwelling) in the River Heights subdivision, in the hope of encouraging others to build. Melson and Wright arrived at a general agreement, and in time, Wright came up with a tentative plan, a drawing of which was published in 1911 in the *Wasmuth Portfolio* (albeit mistakenly labeled).

As it turned out, the timing was unfortunate, to say the least. Before any of this could become a reality, Wright was not only out of the picture in relation to Mason City, but he was literally out of the country as well. The Stockman House had been completed in 1908, and construction of the City National Bank and Park Inn began in April of the following year.

However, as noted earlier, 1909 was the year that Wright's outrageous marital scandal broke, and in late September, he and Mamah Borthwick Cheney left for Europe. Their adultery became publicly known when the story came out (with the headline "Leave Families: Elope to Europe") in the *Chicago Tribune* on November 7, 1909.[180]

Most likely, as Paul Kruty notes, "Melson's—as well as Markley's and Blythe's—rejection of Wright began on that day."[181] Or, as Robert McCoy has said, from that day on, among Mason City residents, Wright was *persona non grata*.[182]

Wright had also become an outcast in his hometown, as architect Richard Neutra found when he arrived in Chicago from Europe:

> *People were flabbergasted that I should have picked up the ideals of a great Chicagoan in a European library, and looked at each other in amazement. ... Wright was not a famous man. He was a terrible man. Had not the Chicago papers brought out lurid stories about him? He had to leave town—and here I was coming from Vienna to look for a person like this and his work!*[183]

Under Construction

Fortunately, even though Wright could no longer oversee the actual construction of the City National Bank and Park Inn, it was reluctantly taken on by his recent associate, Chicago architect William E. Drummond.

Drummond had studied briefly at the University of Illinois School of Architecture. For a short time, he worked for Louis H. Sullivan, then moved on to be the draftsman for some of Wright's most celebrated early projects, including the Cheney residence in Oak Park; the Susan Lawrence Dana House in Springfield, Illinois; and the Larkin Building in Buffalo.

While managing construction of the City National Bank and Park Inn, Drummond took on a sideline assignment (the client was Joshua Melson) to design a speculative residence in the River Heights subdivision, which Melson then sold to Curtis Yelland (a local postal employee and Melson's friend), a structure since referred to as the Yelland House.[184]

Having worked for years with Wright and other Chicago architects, as well as independently, Drummond was undoubtedly well qualified. The posture of the Yelland House is conspicuously horizontal, an effect that is visually reinforced by its pronounced overhanging eaves, lateral wood banding and board and batten siding (a typically vertical feature, as in Grant Wood's *American Gothic*, in this case horizontal).

Almost a century later, the house was all but completely destroyed by a fire in the winter of 2008. Slated for demolition, it was purchased and restored, including the detailed replacement of its built-in interior details.

Wright returned from Europe in October 1910. Less than a month later, on November 5, there was a formal opening of the City National Bank and Park Inn Hotel in Mason City, an event that Wright did not attend.

An article that appeared that day in the *Mason City Times* praised the tandem structure as a "magnificent new building," while it also cautioned that some of the project's components remained unresolved.[185]

Despite his absence from the gala, it was in that same issue of the newspaper that Wright's own account of the building was published (with clear credit to his authorship). As mentioned earlier, this same text was reprinted later in the December 1911 issue of the *Western Architect*.

Regardless of venomous rumors about the sinfulness of the architect, when their bank and hotel were featured with such prominence in a national magazine, "the whole town," Paul Kruty surmises, "must have felt a sense of pride. Modern architecture had taken hold in Mason City."[186]

Meanwhile, Wright's erstwhile building commitment—that of designing a showcase home for Joshua Melson—remained completely in limbo. For whatever reasons, Melson had grown dissatisfied with Wright's proposal (no doubt, he was also disgruntled with Wright), which was a half-hearted adaption of a floor plan that Wright had used previously and that he and others would use as a point of departure again.

Before leaving for Europe, at the last minute, Wright had reached an agreement with another Chicago architect, Herman Von Holst, to temporarily manage his architectural accounts, which included about twenty pending commissions (some of which even lacked drawings).[187]

Mahony's Contribution

In his absence, the bulk of Wright's unfinished work was done by Marion Mahony, who was, as mentioned earlier, one of the first female architects in the country. She was unequaled as a draftsman and had closely worked with Wright for fifteen years. In fact, a substantial number of the drawings in the *Wasmuth Portfolio* are thought to have been made by her (some of which she signed, some not).[188]

To this day, despite her achievements, Marion Mahony Griffin remains largely unheard of, in part because, as the saying goes, her light is usually hidden beneath a bushel basket.[189]

In her case, the basket is twofold: On the one hand, she is outshone by the brightly blinding legend of Frank Lloyd Wright, whose fame she partly enabled. At the same time, her achievements also pale beside the better-known work of her soon-to-be husband, architect Walter Burley Griffin, whose projects she also contributed to, with and without credit.

As often happens in collaborations, especially those of husband and wife (recall, for example, the cooperative works of Gustav Klimt and Emilie Flöge, Charles Rennie Mackintosh and Margaret MacDonald Mackintosh and Charles and Ray Eames), it is frequently unclear which aspects each was responsible for.

Alasdair McGregor views it in this way:

> *Where Walter's pencil stopped and Marion's took over is impossible to say. Architectural creativity, from conceptual sketches through to working drawings and construction detail, should, at its ideal best, be a seamless process, with the finished building the collective and cumulative invention of any number of minds.*[190]

Disadvantaged from the start simply by being a woman (at a time when women's suffrage was a volatile issue), Marion Mahony Griffin was probably also discredited for too freely voicing opinions that were laced with "mordant humor"—a humor that was possibly even more mordant than Wright's.[191]

Lastly, in terms of her being neglected, it probably has not helped that her family name (Mahony not Mahoney) is nearly always misspelled in research articles and books and just as frequently mispronounced (MA-hon-ee, not Ma-HO-NEE), although the Australians, she noted, almost always got it right.[192]

In 1894, the then unmarried Mahony had graduated from the MIT School of Architecture. Soon after, she was hired by her architect cousin, Dwight H. Perkins, to work as an apprentice in Chicago.

Other architects were headquartered in the same building, Frank Lloyd Wright among them, and in 1895, she became Wright's chief (and only) delineator, as well as his first employee.

In that capacity, while working primarily as a draftsman, she also, on occasion, designed furniture, art glass windows (she designed the windows for the Robie House), decorative panels and (while Wright was in Europe) some of the actual buildings themselves. In the year that Wright was absent and too distracted to reply to inquiries, Mahony recalled, "I had great fun designing."[193]

Mahony had been working for Wright for about six years when, in 1901, Wright hired another young Chicago architect named Walter Burley Griffin, who stood out from his colleagues because he was as much devoted to landscape and garden design as to residential architecture. Griffin soon played a prominent part in Wright's studio in Oak Park. His role was especially critical when a project included a garden design, as in the well-known houses for Ward Willets and Darwin Martin.

It appears that working relations between Wright and Walter Burley Griffin were more or less uneventful until 1905, when Wright and his wife, Catherine Tobin Wright (the spouse and mother of his children, whom he would soon abandon), went to Japan for several months, during which Griffin was put in charge of the Oak Park firm.

When Wright returned from Japan in May, he was less than happy with the handling of various matters in his absence. In addition, as was frequently the case, he had run out of money.

Lacking the funds to pay Griffin what he owed him, he instead offered to give Griffin a selection of the Ukiyo-e prints he had purchased on the trip. Griffin protested, but Wright stood by his offer and declared that Griffin's debt had been settled.[194]

Not surprisingly, this did not sit well with Griffin, and by the following spring, he had resigned to start his own architectural firm. Bad blood ensued for many years and eventually led to such bitterness that the two no longer spoke.

At around the same time, a handful of others were working for Wright, among them William Drummond (who would also resign for nonpayment) and Barry Byrne, both of whom, as noted earlier, would soon become key players in the architecture of Mason City.

In addition, Marion Mahony was increasingly indispensable as Wright's chief draftsman, in the course of which she made the drawings for his Mason City projects, including those soon to appear in the *Wasmuth Portfolio*.

In September 1909, just two days after Wright's departure for Europe, she was completing the drawings for the proposed (but later rejected) home that Wright had designed for Joshua Melson on Riverview Heights.

Griffin and Mason City

In the meantime, although Walter Burley Griffin and Marion Mahony were no longer working together in Wright's studio, the two had become a couple. In June 1911, they eloped and married hurriedly, even though Griffin was so beset by deadlines that there was no possibility of a honeymoon.[195]

One cause for his being so busy was that he (with Marion working beside him) was preparing an entry for an international competition for the design of the new federal capital city of Australia, named Canberra.

Given his background in landscape design, Griffin was especially well suited, since the project required not only the design of buildings but also the overall plan of the city itself.

Quite a lot is known about this phase of the Griffins' life because Marion later wrote an autobiography titled "The Magic of America." Never officially published, it has survived as a 1,400-page typescript, supplemented by 650 illustrations.[196]

Throughout that manuscript, she is forthright in her memories of architects and others—and especially of Frank Lloyd Wright, whom she described as an "incubus" whose "malicious vanity" had functioned like a "cancer sore" on Chicago architecture.

In contrast, she had far nicer things to say about Wright's long-suffering client from Mason City, Joshua Melson. He was easily dismayed, so much so that Marion's nickname for him was "Don Melancholio."

One day in 1911, while visiting Chicago, Melson appeared at Marion's place of work, shared his disappointment with Wright's design for Melson's house and talked with her about the possibility that she might prepare a

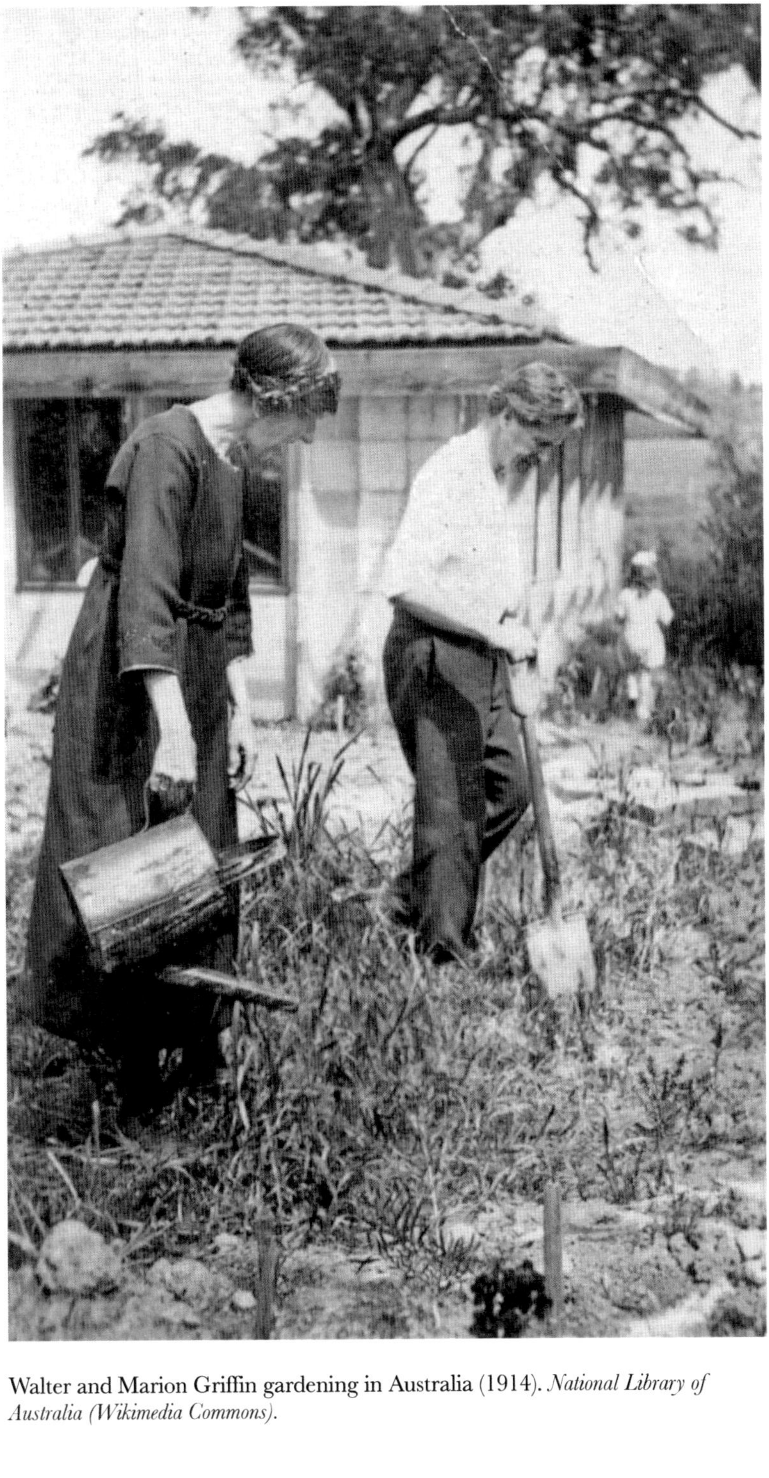

Walter and Marion Griffin gardening in Australia (1914). *National Library of Australia (Wikimedia Commons).*

rendering of the entire riverside neighborhood, which he, Blythe and others were starting to plan.

She responded with moderate interest but then declined the offer. If anything, if they needed a plan for a landscape, she told Melson, they should commission her husband, although he was impossibly busy.[197]

Nevertheless, it all worked out. At some point early in 1912, Walter Burley Griffin traveled to Mason City for the first time to inspect the entire Rock Crest/Rock Glen setting. He talked at length with Melson, Blythe, Markley and other associates about his ideas for the subdivision.

In addition, Griffin and Melson spoke about a new design for Melson's house. It was a breakthrough discussion. Griffin proposed a truly remarkable plan in which (unlike in Wright's proposal), the Melson House would not step back timidly from the edge of the limestone bluff. Rather, it would dramatically and precariously perch on the very edge of the precipice, overlooking the river (and Rock Glen) in the back, while easing in to level land in the front.[198]

Among the most vivid accounts of Griffin's design for the Melson House is that by Alasdair McGregor, in which he describes it as follows:

> *Rather than approaching the cliff on Melson's site as something to be feared and avoided—as if seized by an attack of architectural vertigo—Griffin designed his building to erupt in a burst of vertical rock, all the way from its Silurian foundations. This was no Prairie School expression of ground-hugging horizontality topped with wide eaves and a prominent pitched roof. Instead, in its profound respect for both the terrain and materials garnered from the site, it was a masterly essay in organic design.*[199]

Following Griffin's visit, Melson was all but ecstatic. When her husband returned to Chicago, Marion remembered, he had Don Melancholio Melson "in his pocket." Henceforth, "melancholy flew out and an enduring enthusiasm filled…our Don."[200] What a fortuitous opportunity for both parties. What could possibly go wrong?

ROCK CREST/ROCK GLEN

In the end, what went wrong was what went right. Walter Burley Griffin's design for the Australian federal capital, Canberra, had been one of

137 entries from architects throughout the world. He had prepared it in collaboration with his wife, who made astonishing drawings on linen.

In late May 1912, their submission was awarded the top prize in the Australian competition (among prestigious runners-up was Finnish architect Eliel Saarinen), and suddenly they were locked in to an all-consuming challenge on the other side of the world—one from which Griffin would never return.

When the American architectural community learned that Walter Burley Griffin had won an international competition, his speaking invitations increased. While traveling to those, he continued working on multiple building projects, notably the Stinson Memorial Library in Anna, Illinois, and an ambitious, if sadly ill-fated, community plan for the Trier Center Neighborhood in Winnetka (funded with the prize he won from the Australian competition). Yet somehow Griffin found the time to continue to develop the Mason City project.

In July 1912, he returned to Mason City to confer for several days with Melson and the others. On that trip, he brought with him preliminary drawings for the Melson House, as well as that of Harry D. Page, who had since become part of the project. He also shared with everyone his overall plan for the landscape, the subdivision plots and the locations of all the houses.

Despite the challenge of reaching a group consensus, Griffin and his Mason City clients succeeded in doing just that. They even agreed on the neighborhood's name (most likely Griffin's proposal): it would be officially known as Rock Crest/Rock Glen. Soon after Griffin's departure, the work on the landscape was started, bids were sent out and the actual housing construction began.[201]

The first to be completed was the Page House.[202] It was built in 1912 for a local lumber merchant who had abandoned an earlier house design (proposed by the well-known firm of Purcell and Elmslie in Minneapolis) in compliance with Griffin's request that he alone should have free rein in designing all the houses at the Rock Crest/Rock Glen site.

The second was the structure known as the Arthur Rule House, also completed in 1912.[203] In fact, it was commissioned by law firm partner James E. Blythe, but he lived in it only briefly while awaiting the construction of another more complex residence (also designed by Griffin) in the same neighborhood. When his new home was completed, Blythe sold the earlier one to Rule, who was a partner in the firm.

The third to be completed was a Griffin tour de force. Designed for James E. Blythe himself, it was the largest of the houses and one of the last in which the

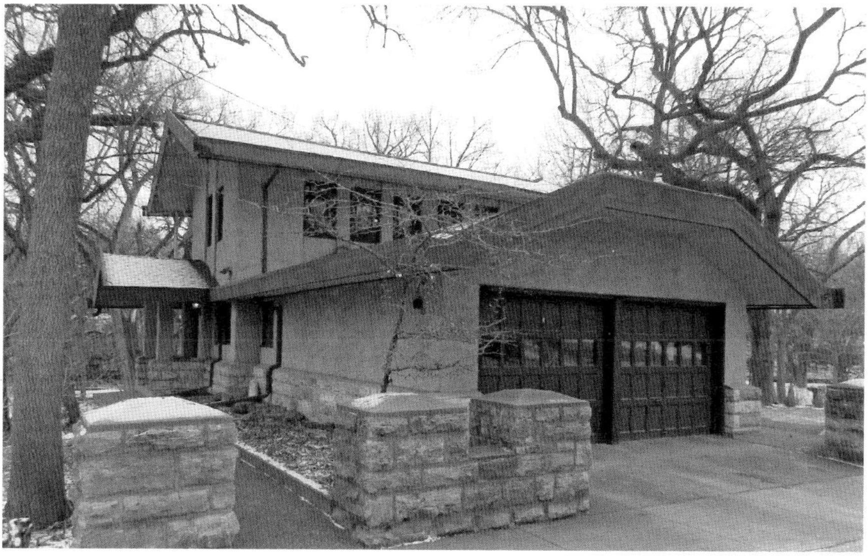

Photograph of the Harry D. Page House in Mason City, in the Rock Crest/Rock Glen neighborhood. *Photograph by Daniel Hartwig (Creative Commons).*

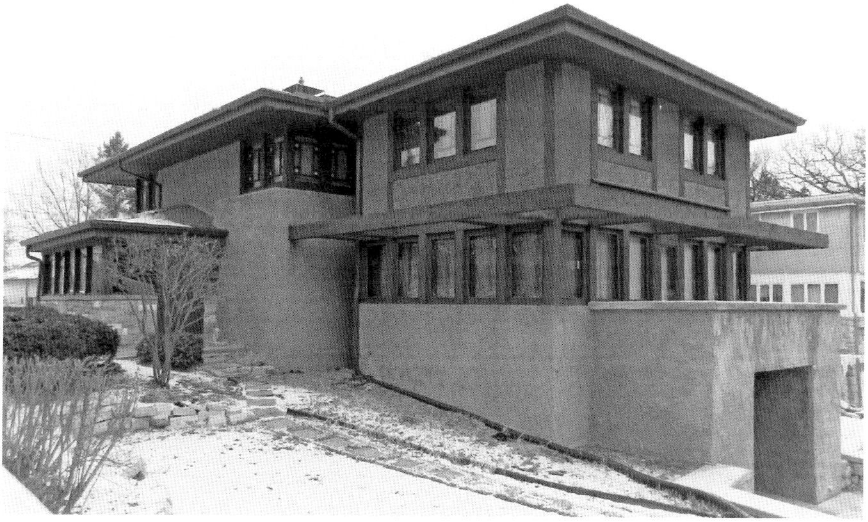

Photograph of the Arthur L. Rule House. *Photograph by Daniel Hartwig (Creative Commons).*

construction was managed by Griffin. It made early innovative use of reinforced concrete, but it also stands apart in terms of architectural style. While well within the look and feel of Prairie School tradition, it has a nuanced resemblance

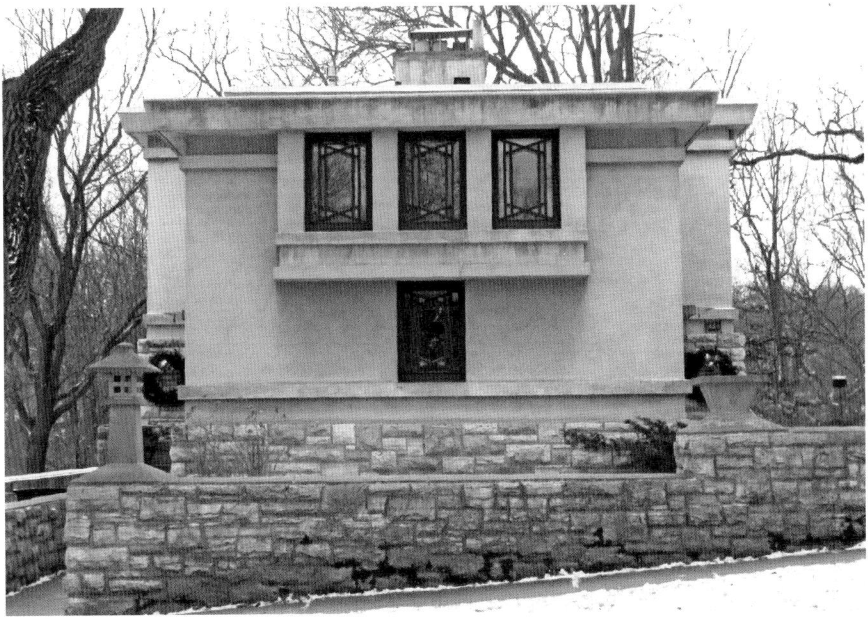

Photograph of the James E. Blythe House in Mason City. *Photograph by Daniel Hartwig (Creative Commons).*

to Meso-American or Mayan architecture. It was the neighborhood's first split-level home. It "stands today," historian H. Allen Brooks has said, "as a significant monument in the annals of American architecture."[204]

Meanwhile, 1913 was a whirlwind year for Walter and Marion Griffin. In the August issue of the *Western Architect* was a thirty-page sequence of drawings, photographs and text on Griffin's recent and in-process projects. It included detailed overviews of his plans for the Trier Center Neighborhood, the architect's own home, the Ricker House (in Grinnell, Iowa), Rock Crest/Rock Glen (in Mason City, including details of the Rule House), Marion Griffin's rendering of the Melson House, a teasing peek at early plans for Canberra and much more.[205] Soon after, his work was featured in the *Architectural Review*.

Australian Obligations

Somewhat earlier, it had also become evident that opposition was growing among conservative Australian officials about Griffin's plan for Canberra.

He agreed to travel to Sydney for a few weeks to look more closely at the site. He arrived there in August 1913 and, in the end, extended his stay for several months.

By the time Griffin left Australia in November, those who opposed his plan had been (ineffectively) silenced, and in an awkward power struggle, he had been appointed the federal capital director of design and construction. Under contract, he agreed to return to Australia in a few months to resume his supervisory work and to remain there for about three years.

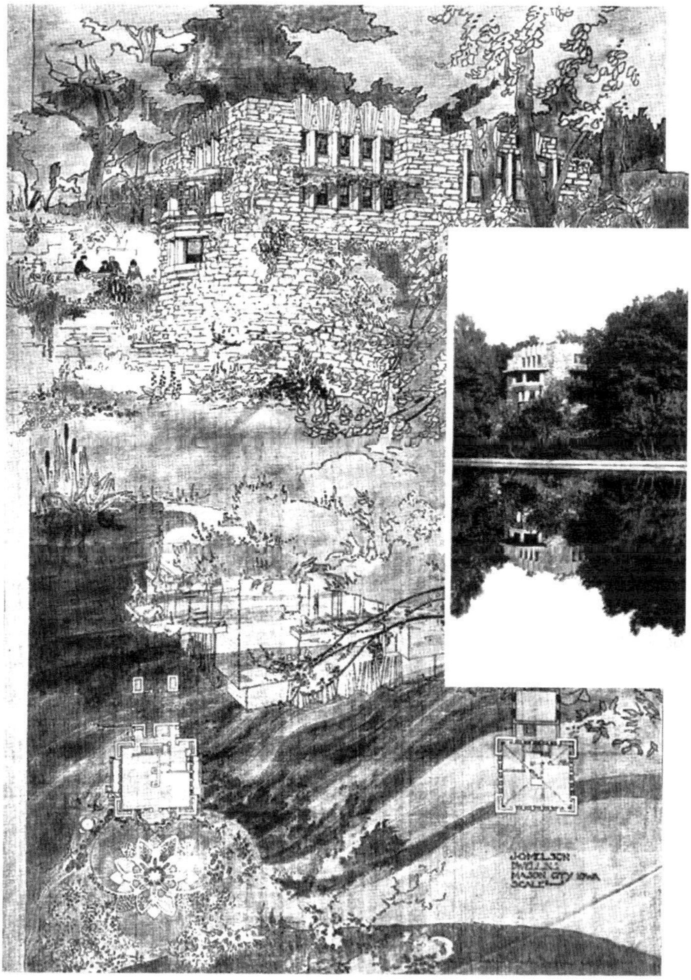

Marion Mahony Griffin's rendering of her husband's design for the Joshua G. Melson House, as published in the *Western Architect* (August 1913).

Arriving back in Chicago by mid-December, Griffin had only two weeks before he was due in Mason City for a meeting with his Rock Crest/Rock Glen clients. Although he didn't know it, it would be his final meeting with them.[206]

He had been all but unknown on the two occasions when he had visited Mason City before. Now, as the recipient of an international award, he was a celebrity. He was given top-rank coverage in local news reports. He even got undeserved credit when the newspaper mistakenly mentioned that he (not Frank Lloyd Wright) had designed the City National Bank and Park Inn.

At the time of that visit, the Melson House was nearly completed, and the Blythe House was under construction. The visit was largely a formality and included the presentation of gifts from the architect to his clients. It is interesting to learn (recalling Wright's bungled relations with Griffin) that Griffin's gift to the Blythes was a selection of Japanese Ukiyo-e prints.[207]

As for Melson, he could not have been happier. His house was attracting attention, just as he had always hoped. Townspeople had begun calling it "The Castle" (some Mason City residents still refer to it as that).

Later, Marion Mahony Griffin recalled the day when Melson ("the old 'sad face'") showed up again at the Chicago office "saying that he was going to have to charge up his electric bills to Mr. Griffin"—and then he laughed—because "everyone, and that was the whole town [of Mason City], who crossed the bridge...whether pedestrian or motorist, stopped to look up the river at the fascinating sight of Rock Crest's initial building." As a result, she continued, Melson "couldn't resist the temptation of keeping his whole house lighted up to make the most of a spectacle of it."[208]

During this final visit to Mason City (in late December 1913), Griffin explained to Melson that he and Marion were leaving soon for Europe—specifically, Vienna—to meet the famous secessionist architect Otto Wagner.[209]

Would Melson like to come along?

Melson agreed, and from all reports, it was a pleasurable escapade. (It's not clear if they were accompanied by Millie Melson, Melson's wife, who was suffering from heart trouble and would die of a stroke in 1915.)

At the conclusion of that venture, the Griffins returned to Chicago, then departed for Australia in mid-April, arriving there in early May.

However, before he could leave for Australia, Griffin was faced with the problem of finding someone who would be willing—and able—to manage his Chicago architectural firm during his anticipated three-year absence. After considering various options, he made an offer to Chicago architect Barry Byrne, a former Griffin co-worker who had also been a draftsman for Frank Lloyd Wright.

Byrne had relocated to Los Angeles, where he was less than happy. He accepted Griffin's offer, and the name of the patchwork firm became Griffin and Byrne. Byrne then moved back to Chicago, where the mutual expectation was that, in Griffin's absence, he would carry out Griffin's intentions for his ongoing projects. If any significant problems arose, Griffin would be consulted.

Agreement Deteriorates

The Griffins soon left for Australia, and for a short time, things were uneventful at the Chicago office. Unfortunately, Griffin had not realized the extent of Byrne's continued loyalty to Wright.

When Wright expressed annoyance to Byrne about his new partnership with Griffin (to whom Wright was no longer speaking), Byrne answered that his greatest dread was that he, too, would end up on Wright's list of enemies. His commitments to Griffin, he reassured Wright, were secondary and merely a "business" arrangement.[210]

Only months after the Griffins' departure for Australia, apparent lapses began to occur in the implementation of Griffin and Byrne's agreement. As time passed, Byrne's updates all but ceased, and in some cases, substantial changes in buildings were made without Griffin's knowledge.

To be sure, Griffin's workload in Australia was such (he had faced bitter opposition to his ambitious city plan) that he could not possibly micromanage the Chicago office—after all, that's what Byrne was hired to do.

Back in Mason City, a familiar figure returned to the stage. It was Charles H. MacNider, the prominent businessman, banker and longtime competitor of Markley and Blythe. A few years earlier, he had built the new eight-story First National Bank, perhaps in part as a challenge to Wright's City National Bank and Park Inn. In a few years hence, he would also build the Hanford Hotel, which all but ensured the certain decline of the Park Inn.[211]

Soon after Griffin's departure for Australia, MacNider approached Byrne about remodeling his own mansion, a house in the Greek Revival style.[212] Byrne agreed to do so, although in style and philosophy the structure was the inverse of Prairie School architecture.[213] While it was Byrne's decision to take this project on, the remodeled house was credited to the firm of Griffin and Byrne. Yet he never mentioned it to Griffin.

A further complication was that Byrne began to have personal differences with a client who had reached an earlier agreement with Griffin.

That client, Samuel Davis Drake, wanted a Prairie School home in the Rock Crest/Rock Glen neighborhood.[214] He had purchased land on Rock Crest from Melson, and Griffin had supplied the plans.

However, with Griffin in Australia, Byrne soon concluded that Drake was impossible to work with, and he chose to cancel the project. There may have been good reason for this—but apparently, once again, he failed to let his partner know.

In search of a new architect, Drake approached a Mason City firm called J.H. Jeffers and Company. The person on the company's staff in charge of Drake's house project was a Scandinavian immigrant, a somewhat furtive architect named Einar Broaten. Broaten's firm, as well as his client, was greatly pleased with the Prairie School result of the Drake House. Broaten became a partner, and the firm was soon renamed Jeffers and Broaten.[215]

Broaten was born in Norway in 1884 and appears to have come to the United States prior to 1912. He was active as an architect in Mason City and nearby Iowa communities for at least a dozen years, until 1924. It is believed that he designed about thirteen buildings in Mason City, Clear Lake, Hanlontown, Garner, Hampton, Sheffield and West Bend, many of which are exemplary of Prairie School architecture.

In *Buildings of Iowa*, David Gebhard and Gerald Mansheim conclude of Broaten that, if in fact he did design the houses attributed to him, he "should be placed within the front ranks of the Prairie movement."[216]

Regarding Broaten, it is an awkward coincidence (as noted by Kruty) that the offices of the Jeffers firm were located in none other than Charles H. MacNider's First National Bank building. The same source also mentions that, at some point, when Broaten's Drake House was featured in a magazine, it was mistakenly credited to Frank Lloyd Wright.[217]

It is sometimes rumored that Einar Broaten's potential as an architect was eventually undermined by a recurrent health issue. For whatever reason, Broaten left Mason City in 1927 and moved to Fergus Falls, Minnesota. There he formed an architectural firm called Broaten and Foss with Magnus O. Foss (whose architect father had also immigrated from Norway). In February 1948, at age sixty-three, Broaten was reported missing. Nine weeks later, his body was found beneath a bridge in the river in Fergus Falls.[218]

Limits of Modernism

If the halcyon days of modern-era buildings in Mason City can be said to have begun in 1908 with the arrival of Frank Lloyd Wright, it might also be said that they started to fade as early as 1917, in the year America entered World War I.

Recalling what happened in subsequent years, it's clear that Wright's three buildings (the Stockman House, City National Bank and Park Inn) were at

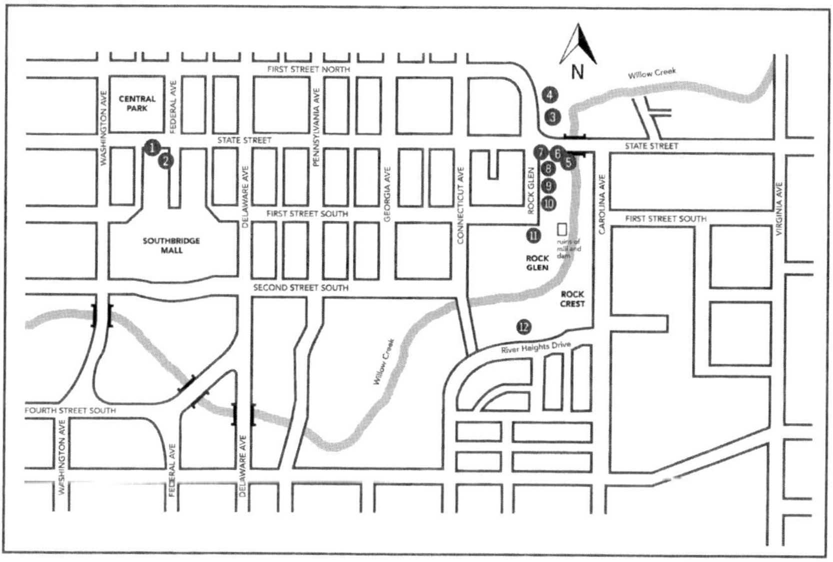

This street map of downtown Mason City, Iowa, shows the locations of its major historic Prairie School buildings. At the top left is Central Park. At the turn of the nineteenth century, Federal Avenue was known as Main Street, and the city's busiest intersection was at State Street and Main. The three buildings designed by Frank Lloyd Wright are the Park Inn Hotel (1), the City National Bank (2) and the Stockman House (3), shown in its current location (having been carefully moved and restored).

Adjacent to the Stockman House Museum is the Robert E. McCoy Architectural Interpretive Center (4). By walking south across State Street, one enters the two-pronged neighborhood that was planned by Walter Burley Griffin, with its two sides bordering Willow Creek.

The lower side is called Rock Glen, while the side overlooking the bluffs is called Rock Crest. The houses on State Street in Rock Glen include the Sam Schneider House (5), the Hugh Gilmore House (6) and the E.V. Francke House (7). Walking south on Rock Glen Lane, one finds the Arthur Rule House (8), the Tom MacNider House (9) and the Harry Page House (10). Continuing to the corner of Rock Glen Lane and First Street Southeast, there is the James Blythe House (11), from which one can see across Willow Creek to the limestone bluffs of Rock Crest, on top of which is Griffin's conspicuous masterpiece, the Joshua G. Melson House (12). Other significant dwellings are found throughout the city, some of which were designed by other Prairie School architects, among them William Drummond and Einar Broaten. *Author's diagram.*

times in danger of being destroyed or ruined through remodeling. As for the Rock Crest/Rock Glen houses, while not threatened by demolition, they, too, were sometimes compromised by remodeling. Meanwhile, the Rock Crest/Rock Glen development always fell short of Griffin's original plans.[219]

Initially, Griffin had anticipated the inclusion of nineteen houses.[220] In the end, only seven of those were built, all single-family dwellings. Five had been designed by Griffin (the Page, Rule, Melson, Blythe and Schneider Houses). Two others (Gilmore and Francke), while part of the project, were largely designed by Barry Byrne, with allegedly less than full regard for the initial ideas of Griffin, who was in Australia by then.

There are other houses that might also be included. Among these are the Drake House (designed by Broaten) on Rock Crest and, in Rock Glen, the Tom MacNider House.[221] The latter, designed some forty years later (in 1959) by Wright associate Curtis Besinger, is not strictly a Prairie School house but closer to what Wright would eventually call Usonian. And there is, of course, the Yelland House, designed by William Drummond.

In the long view of Griffin's achievements, it should come as no surprise to learn that the house in Mason City that stands above the others (not only literally) is the Melson House. As H. Allen Brooks has said, it is "a master stroke" in which Griffin "turned the cliff to his advantage," with the result that the building is "partly hewn, [and] partly growing from the

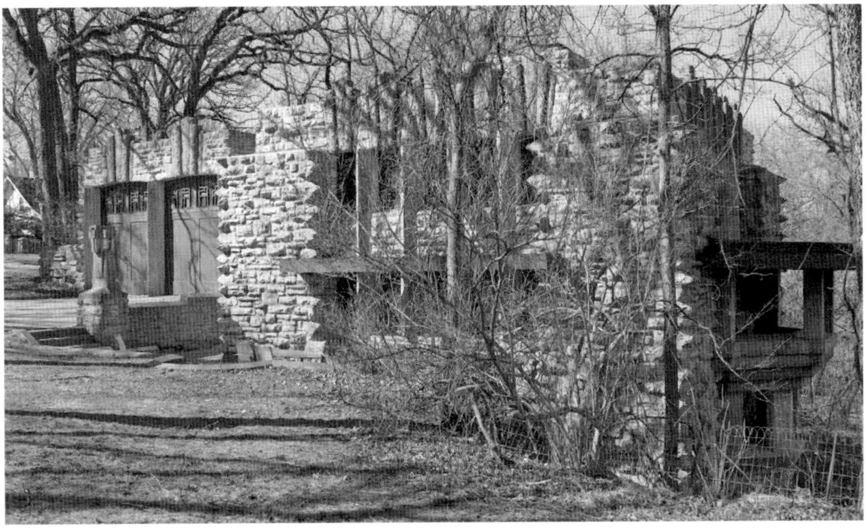

The Melson House in its current restored state (2016). Note the interplay of shadows. *Author's photograph.*

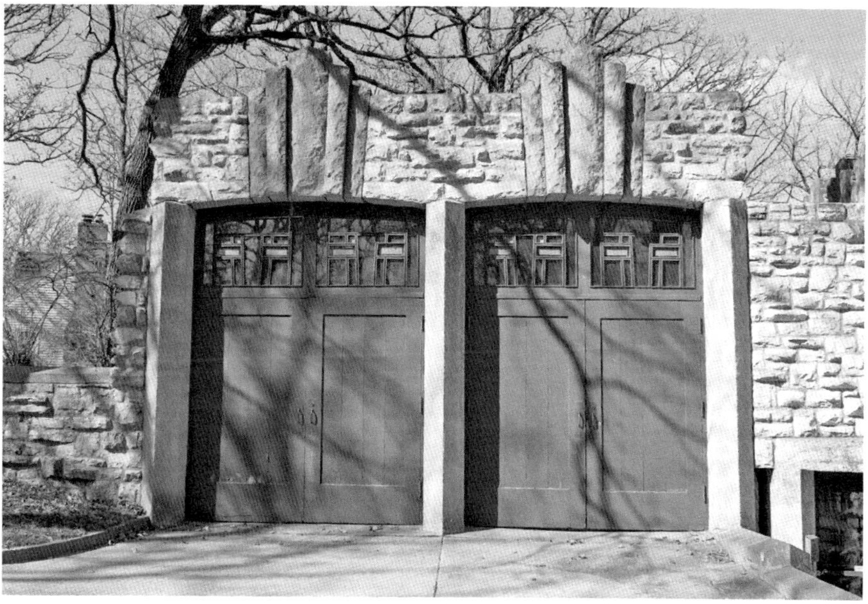

The drive-through garage for the Melson House, on the front side of the house, has two pairs of doors, eliminating the need to back up. *Author's photograph.*

striated cliff."[222] Amazingly, as Hurley notes, "although the almost fortress-like structure appears to be part of the cliff face, the interior is open and spacious, human in its scale, proportions, and liveability."[223]

In addition, the Melson House comes with exuberant tales, some of them even more colorful than Don Melancholio's mood swings. For example, it is said that Griffin, when the building's outside walls were done, celebrated by climbing (rock by rock) to the roof of the building from the banks of the river below it.[224]

In another anecdote, there are photographs that confirm that a one-time owner of the Melson House decided in the 1950s that it would look more attractive if pink paint were applied to the outside wooden trim and the concrete mullions.[225]

When the lurid result was photographed and published, it somehow reached Australia. Some years later, when an American photographer traveled to Australia to document Griffin's stone-walled houses there, he found that some of the owners had added the same pink to their own Griffin homes, thinking that Griffin had planned it that way.[226]

Fortunately, this astonishing structure was purchased in 1994 by new owners (Roger and Peggy Bang) and painstakingly restored.

Designing for Nature

In 1914, the very same year the Griffins arrived, Australia entered World War I. While opposition to Griffin's plan for Canberra was fueled by ferocious political strife, there were also reassessments of the government's priorities and resulting funding cuts. There were even wartime suspicions expressed about Griffin's non-Australian status, as well as his past admiration for the work of German architects.

Prior to settling there, the Griffins had nothing but admiration for Australia and its people. But having lived there for a year, their views were radically reversed. As James Weirick has described it:

> *Caught in a complex web of jealousy, intrigue, indifference and misunderstanding, played out against the social hysteria of Australia during the First World War, their* [the Griffins'] *faith in Australia as a rational, modern society was deeply shaken.*[227]

By 1918, Griffin was at wit's end. He was distressed by the endless delays and fierce opposition to most of his plans. It was even suspected that bureaucrats had purposely supplied him with incorrect data as a way to undermine his work.[228]

He resigned soon after and (along with other projects) turned instead to a new, long-term proposal that resembled his previous (and largely unsuccessful) attempts to build planned communities—the Trier Center Neighborhood in Winnetka and the Rock Crest/Rock Glen neighborhood in Mason City.

In 1920, the Griffins formed a company called the Greater Sydney Development Association (GSDA), with which they were able to purchase 650 acres of undeveloped land in Sydney Harbor, four miles of which bordered the water. From the outset, their plan was to gradually build up an unprecedented community in which the Australian bush and innovative house designs would coexist harmoniously, where buildings and the landscape merge.

There would be "no boundaries, [and] no fences," and roads and footpaths would comply with the byways already implied by the contours of the land. A master at choosing evocative names, Griffin christened it Castlecrag.[229]

Not surprisingly, given the emboldened blending between the house and limestone bluff in Mason City's Melson House, Griffin's Castlecrag designs have much in common with that earlier project. Of the forty-five houses that Griffin designed for Castlecrag (fifteen of which were actually built), one that is frequently cited as among the most successful is the Fishwick House.

Built in 1929, the Fishwick House was made of the stone from its surroundings. Its appearance, at times, is that of a cave rather than a

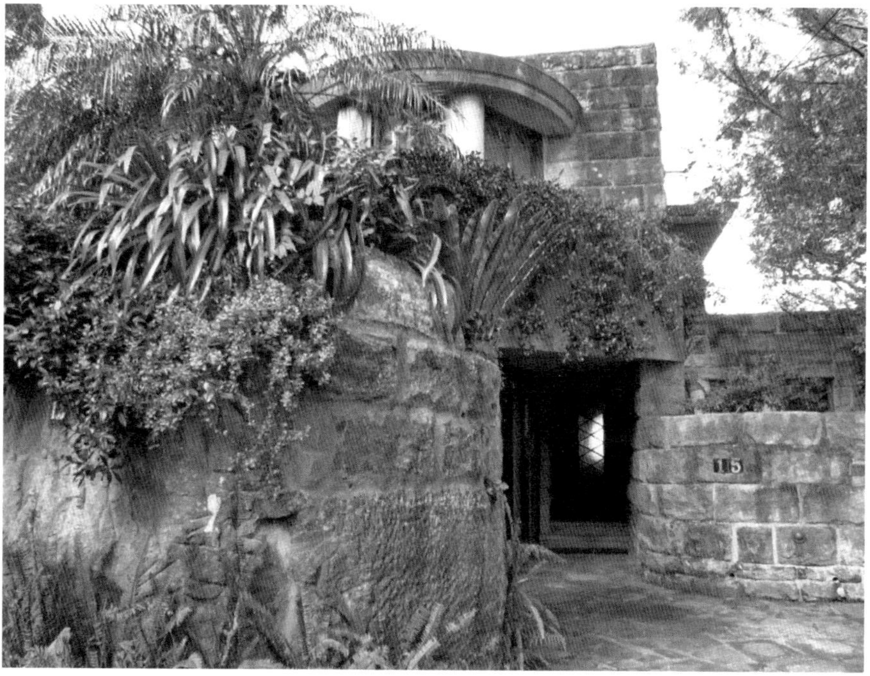

Walter Burley Griffin's design for the Fishwick House in Castlecrag, near Sydney, Australia. *Photograph courtesy Ian Tocher ©2012. Used with permission.*

dominant, conspicuous home, albeit inside it is lavish and large. Like the Melson House, the impression is that it grew out of the land, that the two are inseparable (or at least wholly compatible), in stark contrast to the prevalent goal of agrarian conquest.

Both the Melson House and Fishwick House are exemplars of the practice of Griffin's belief in "designing for nature," whereby a building ought to be (in his words) "the logical outgrowth of the environment in which [it is] located."[230]

As Frank Lloyd Wright would later say, "No house should ever be on a hill. It should be of the hill. Belonging to it."[231] As do other Griffin designs, the Melson and Fishwick Houses anticipate Wright's evocation of a later parallel approach, when he designed Fallingwater (the Kaufmann House) in 1936.

Death in India

In the same year, on the other side of the world, the Griffins left Australia for India, where Walter had been asked to design a major university library. He soon had a flood of commissions, and he grew increasingly interested in the possibilities of contributing to the modern architecture of that exotic country.

Tragically, while in India, Walter Burley Griffin grew terribly ill. It was soon determined that his gall bladder had ruptured, and he was taken in for surgery. Five days later, he died in the hospital of peritonitis. Marion was at his bedside at the end.

As she later recalled in a letter to her sister:

> *As his breath began to fail, I talked to him, told him what a wonderful life I had had with him, how he was beloved by everybody and suddenly*

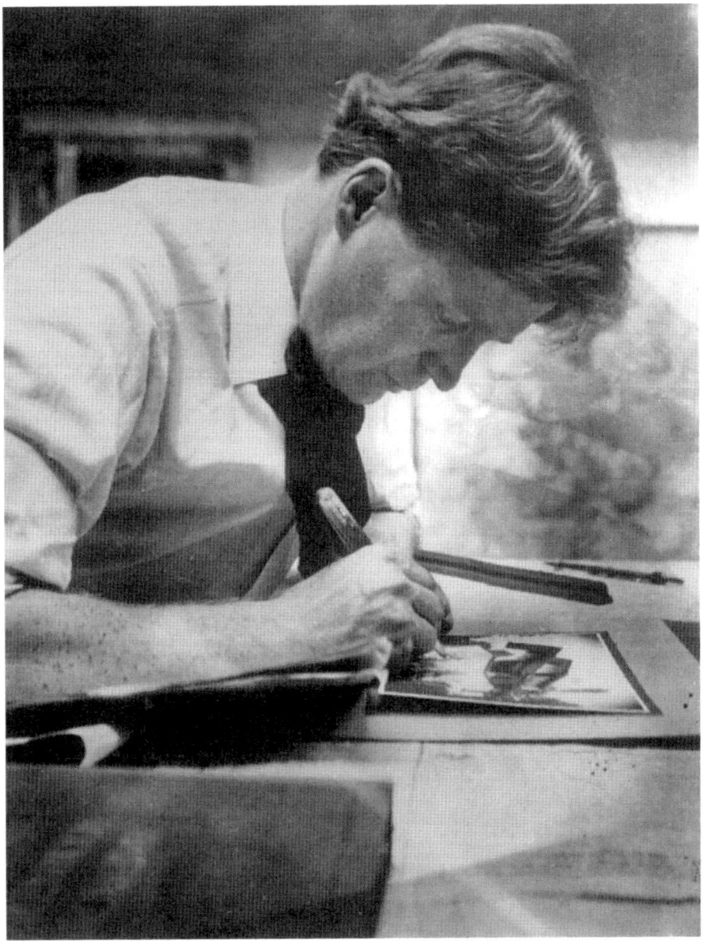

American architect Walter Burley Griffin, as photographed in 1912. *State Library of New South Wales, Australia.*

> *he turned and fastened his eyes wide open and round on mine, startled and intense as if it had never occurred to him that he could die and they never left mine till he ceased breathing and I closed them.*[232]

Following the death of her husband, Marion Mahony Griffin declined the opportunity to continue his work in India. She moved back to Chicago instead, reestablished family ties and tried to continue to practice as an architect. She described her husband's and her life at considerable length in "The Magic of America." She died in 1961.

The ill-fated agreement between Griffin and Barry Byrne was dissolved in 1917. Unable to return to the United States, it had taken Griffin years to learn the truth about activities at the Chicago office.

Years later, when Byrne was interviewed by Studs Terkel in *Division Street*, he appeared on the brink of confessing to some measure of malevolence. "I've always been guilty of a certain artistic snobbism," he said, "like pushing out of sight all the members of the Prairie School when I got to know Wright. Because they didn't fly as high as he. Only these last years, remembering my boyhood, I can see how unjust I was to all these people."[233] Byrne died the year Terkel's book came out, when he was struck by an automobile.

Wright Lives On

As for Frank Lloyd Wright's career, it continued for years, unabated. In 1937, the year that Walter Burley Griffin died (at age sixty), Wright was close to seventy. Wright would not only live for two more decades, but he would also go on to produce important buildings. For example, if he had died at Griffin's age, he would not have designed the Guggenheim Museum, the Price Tower, Wingspread, the V.C. Morris Gift Shop, the Monona Terrace Center and the majority of his Usonian homes.

Looking back on Wright's brief connection with Mason City (in total, he was probably present in the town for only a few days), a pesky, unresolved puzzle remains. As mentioned earlier, Wright was able to oversee the construction of the Stockman House in 1908. He also finished the blueprints for the City National Bank and Park Inn, which then opened formally on November 5, 1910.

However, because of the outrageous scandal about his elopement to Europe with Mamah Borthwick Cheney in October 1909, he was unable to manage the construction of those buildings, nor did he attend the opening of the bank and hotel (although he was back from Europe by then).

In the absence of proof to the contrary, it is usually assumed that Wright never returned to Mason City after 1909, so that, although he had access to photographs of the finished buildings, he never saw the structures themselves.

And if by chance he did return to Mason City after 1926, how would he have reacted to the momentous alterations done to the City National Bank or the deterioration of the Park Inn Hotel?

Related to this, posted on the Internet in recent years (as part of a Bonham's online auction) was a postcard, of which only the message side was shown, handwritten and signed by Frank Lloyd Wright.[234]

It is dated February 15, 1941, and is clearly addressed to Mason City lawyer James E.E. Markley (Wright's former client), who was one of those who hired him to design the bank and hotel.

The message on the postcard reads: "On March 13th I will be in Mason City. Please be my guest on February 14th [*sic*] for dinner at the Hotel. I will look forward to seeing you."

There are several peculiarities in this message. One is a presumed error on the date of the dinner (he apparently meant to say "March 14th" instead of "February 14th").

Another question has to do with the dinner's location. When Wright says "hotel," is he talking about the Park Inn (one would think so, given Markley's and his historic involvement with that), or does he mean the Hanford Hotel (regarded then as the city's upscale place to stay)?

The third problem with the postcard is that Wright is obviously unaware that Markley is no longer living. He had died two years earlier, on October 19, 1939, at age eighty-two.

Why was Wright planning to be in Mason City? Was he merely driving through? Was he meeting with a client in Mason City? Was he wanting—if only out of curiosity—to return to see the physical state of the tandem building(s) that he had designed some thirty years earlier?

In the end, we are left to wonder if, at some moment, Wright actually stood in the presence of the bank and hotel that he had conceived of and produced in 1908.

For this and other reasons, the enigma of Frank Lloyd Wright endures. As do—thanks to the efforts of Mason City citizens—the magnificent, now-restored structures themselves.

MASON CITY AND PRAIRIE SCHOOL ARCHITECTURE

A Chronology

1844	Richard Lloyd Jones and his family emigrate from Cardiganshire, Wales, to Union (now Ixonia), Wisconsin.
1846	Iowa Territory is granted statehood.
1851	Founding of Cerro Gordo County (named for a prominent battle in the Mexican-American War in 1847) in north-central Iowa, with an initial population of eight Euro-Americans.
1851	Crystal Palace Exhibition opens (first World's Fair) in Hyde Park, London.
1852	Death of kindergarten founder Friedrich Froebel.
1852	Publication of *Uncle Tom's Cabin* by Harriet Beecher Stowe.
1853	Mason City is established (originally known as Shibboleth, then Mason Grove).
1853	Commodore Matthew Perry arrives in Tokyo Bay with heavily armed black ships; demands trade negotiations with Japan.
1854	Lloyd Jones and his family move from Ixonia to Jones Valley, near Spring Green, Wisconsin.
1854	The first physician arrives in Mason City.
1854	Transcendentalist Henry David Thoreau publishes *Walden*.

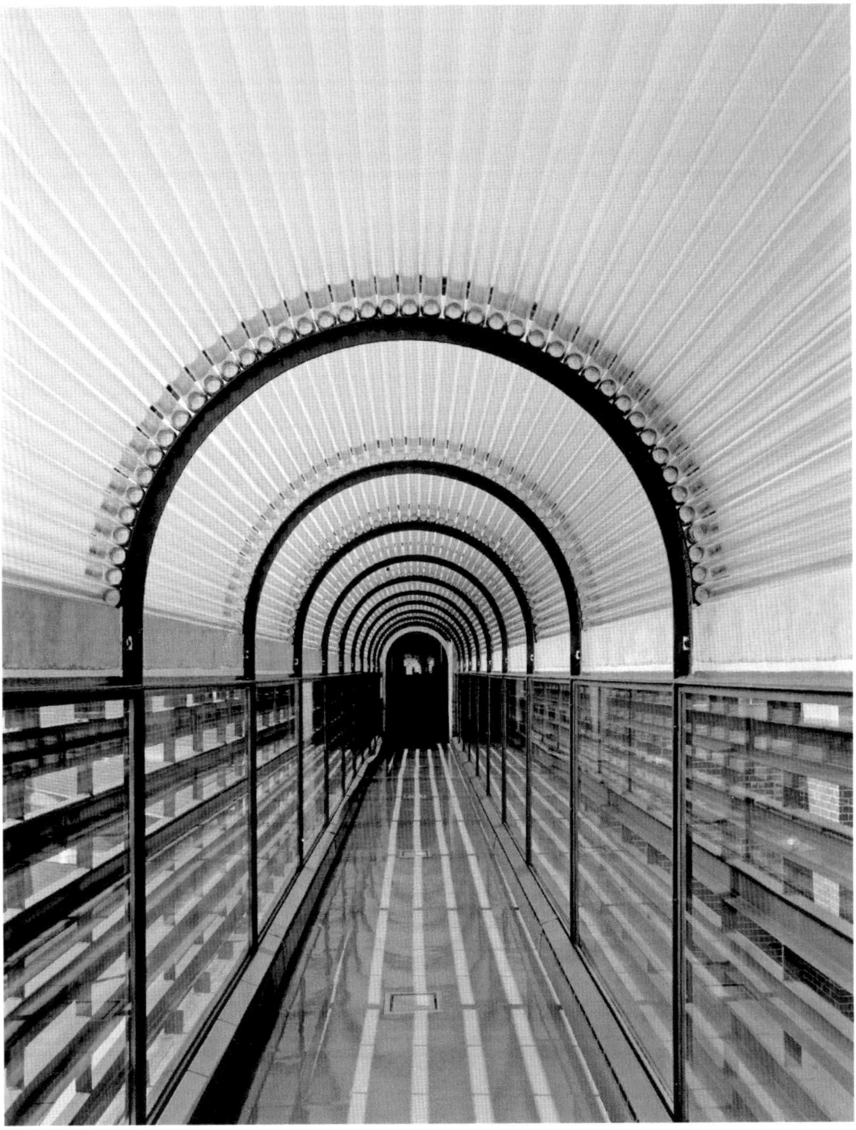

Corridor designed by Wright at the Johnson Wax Corporation Building. Photograph by Carol M. Highsmith (n.d.). *Carol M. Highsmith Archive, LOC Prints and Photographs.*

1854 Inter-tribal conflicts among Native Americans near Clear Lake, Iowa (called the Grindstone War) prompt temporary evacuation of the area's Euro-American settlers.

1855 First sawmill erected near Mason City on Lime Creek. Also established that year are the city's first grocery store, law office, blacksmith shop and photography studio.

1855 American poet Walt Whitman publishes his collection of poems *Leaves of Grass*.

1856 Birth of architect Louis H. Sullivan in Boston.

1856 Publication in London of Owen Jones's *The Grammar of Ornament*.

1856 Educator Margarethe Meyer-Schurz (wife of statesman and reformer Carl Schurz) starts the first Froebel kindergarten in the United States in Watertown, Wisconsin.

1856 Abolitionist John Brown and followers murder five slavery supporters in the Pottawatomie Massacre in Kansas.

1856 First school in Mason City begins in a log cabin, prompting construction of the first stone school building the following year.

1857 About thirty-five Euro-American settlers are attacked and killed (called the Spirit Lake Massacre) by a group of Santee Sioux Native Americans near Spirit Lake, Iowa, one hundred miles west of Mason City.

1858 Mason City is designated the county seat of Cerro Gordo County.

1858 *Cerro Gordo Press*, the first Mason City newspaper, begins publication.

1859 John Brown leads an unsuccessful raid on the U.S. Arsenal at Harpers Ferry, West Virginia.

1859 Charles Darwin publishes *On the Origin of the Species*.

1861 With the attack on Fort Sumter in Charleston, South Carolina, the American Civil War begins.

1861 British designer, poet and social reformer William Morris co-founds an interior design firm, later called Morris and Company. His efforts will establish him as the leading figure in the arts and crafts movement.

1862 At Mankato, Minnesota, thirty-eight Santee Sioux Native American men are put to death by mass hanging for attacks on Euro-Americans. It is the largest group execution in U.S. history.

1864	In Colorado Territory, a camp of as many as 160 peaceful Cheyenne and Arapaho Native Americans (two-thirds women and children) are killed and mutilated by a 700-man militia of Euro-American soldiers in what is known as the Sand Creek Massacre.
1864	First millinery shop opens in Mason City.
1865	American Civil War ends with the surrender of the Confederate army on April 9. In the same month, U.S. president Abraham Lincoln is assassinated.
1865	First lumberyard opens in Mason City.
1867	Birth of Frank Lincoln Wright (name later changed to Frank Lloyd Wright) in Richland Center, Wisconsin.
1869	Completion in Utah of the link between the Union Pacific and Central Pacific railway lines, the country's first transcontinental railroad.
1869	The Milwaukee Road railroad line to Mason City is completed, and the first train arrives in the city.
1869	First Mason City bank (Cerro Gordo County Bank) is founded.
1870	Milwaukee Road railway is extended to Austin, Minnesota. Completion of an additional Iowa Central railroad line to Mason City is eventually followed by others.
1870	A second mill is constructed on Willow Creek at Mason City.
1871	Birth of Marion Mahony in Chicago.
1871	In the Great Chicago Fire, much of the downtown business community is destroyed. The family of infant Marion Mahony flees to Hubbard Woods, north of Chicago, where they resettle in Winnetka, Illinois.
1871	The first brickyard opens in Mason City.
1872	Completion of the Brooklyn Bridge.
1876	Births of architects Walter Burley Griffin in Maywood, Illinois, and William Drummond in Newark, New Jersey.
1876	Mark Twain publishes *Tom Sawyer*.
1876	Wright's mother attends the Centennial World's Fair in Philadelphia. After learning about kindergarten, she brings home a set of Froebel's wooden blocks.

1876	Throughout the United States, Euro-Americans are alarmed and shocked to learn that the Seventh Cavalry, under the command of General George A. Custer, has been defeated by Native Americans (presumed to be an inferior race) at the Battle of Little Big Horn.
1877	Thomas Edison invents the phonograph.
1878	First telephone system installed in Mason City.
1879	Edison invents the electric light bulb.
1880	New York City installs electric streetlights.
1883	Jenkin Lloyd Jones (Frank Lloyd Wright's "Uncle Jenk") founds the All Souls Unitarian Church in Chicago.
1883	Completion of the Parker Opera House in downtown Mason City on Federal Avenue, across from the northeast corner of Central Park.
1883	Birth of architect Barry Byrne in Chicago.
1884	The City Bank (later renamed the City National Bank) is founded, with Thomas Emsley as president. When he dies two years later, his wife, Mary Church Emsley, a major shareholder, becomes the new bank president.
1884	Dedication of the Iowa State Capitol Building in Des Moines.
1884	Civil War monument erected in Central Park in Mason City.
1884	Mark Twain publishes *The Adventures of Huckleberry Finn*.
1884	The linotype machine is patented.
1884	The first skyscraper is built in Chicago.
1886	Frank Lloyd Wright joins Joseph Silsbee's Chicago architectural firm.
1886	Joseph Silsbee designs Unity Chapel in Spring Green, Wisconsin, with Frank Lloyd Wright as draftsman.
1886	The Statue of Liberty is dedicated.
1886	Streetlights are installed in Mason City.
1887	Wright joins the Chicago firm of Adler and Sullivan as draftsman.

1888	Lilly Emsley, daughter of Mary Church Emsley, marries Mason City lawyer James E.E. Markley, who will later recommend Wright as the architect for the new City National Bank. A Unitarian and outspoken women's rights advocate, Mary Emsley is well acquainted with Wright's uncle Jenkin Lloyd Jones, a prominent Chicago-based Unitarian preacher.
1890	Scholar Ernest Fenollosa (cousin of Joseph Silsbee) is named to the curatorial staff of the new Japanese department at the Boston Museum of Fine Arts.
1892	Inventor John Froelich develops the first gasoline-powered tractor in Waterloo, Iowa.
1892	Mason City Brick and Tile Company is founded.
1893	Wright is fired by Sullivan for moonlighting; he begins his own architectural firm.
1893	Birth of arts impresario and book designer Merle Armitage in Mason City.
1896	First Ford automobile.
1896	U.S. mail delivery is provided to farms through the Rural Free Delivery Act.
1899	Publication of Arthur Wesley Dow's *Composition*.
1899	Jacob Decker purchases the Mason City slaughterhouse and begins the Decker Meat Packing Plant.
1902	Birth of composer and playwright Meredith Willson in Mason City.
1902	Wright designs a new building for his aunts' Hillside Home School near Spring Green. In the same year, Marion Markley, the eldest granddaughter of Mary Church Emsley, enrolls in the school and is soon followed by her younger sister, Doris. In visiting the school, their parents, James and Lillie Markley, are impressed by the building's architecture.
1903	Wright designs the office building of the Larkin Soap Company in Buffalo, New York.
1903	Construction of the Wilson Opera House in Mason City, near the northwest corner of Central Park.
1903	Orville and Wilbur Wright make the first sustained airplane flight at Kitty Hawk.

1905	Mason City Carnegie Library opens.
1905	Albert Einstein publishes *The Theory of Relativity*.
1906	Wright designs the Robie House in Chicago.
1906	Publication of Kakuzo Okakura's *The Book of Tea*.
1906	First motion picture theater arrives in Mason City.
1908	Founding of Northwestern States Portland Cement Company in Mason City. After a financially troubled beginning, it is taken over in 1911 and thereafter productively managed by banker Charles H. MacNider.
1908	Construction of the Stockman House in Mason City, designed by Frank Lloyd Wright.
1910	Construction of the City National Bank and Park Inn in Mason City, designed by Wright.
1911	Lehigh Portland Cement Company of Allentown, Pennsylvania, establishes a Mason City facility.
1911	Marriage of Walter Burley Griffin and Marion Mahony.
1912	Completion of the Arthur Rule and Harry Page Houses in Mason City, designed by Walter Burley Griffin.
1913	Walter and Marion Griffin relocate to Australia, expecting to remain there for about three years.
1914	Completion of the James E. Blythe and Joshua Melson Houses in Mason City, designed by Walter Burley Griffin.
1914	Mamah Borthwick Cheney (Wright's partner), her two children and others at Talisesin, near Spring Green, Wisconsin, perish in an attack and subsequent arson by a house servant.
1914	Wright designs Midway Gardens in Chicago.
1915	Completion of the Sam Schneider House, designed by Walter Burley Griffin, and the Hugh Gilmore House by Barry Byrne in Mason City.
1917	United States enters World War I. Soon after, the governor of Iowa forbids the use in public of any non-English language by people in groups of two or more.
1917	Completion of the E.V. Franke House, designed by Barry Byrne, in Mason City.
1919	Radios are introduced in Iowa homes.

1921	In Australia, Walter Burley Griffin and the Greater Sydney Development Association become owners of ninety acres of rocky terrain. This will become the location of a Griffin-planned community called Castlecrag.
1922	Operations begin in Mason City at the Northern Sugar Corporation.
1923	Completion of the Imperial Hotel in Tokyo, designed by Wright. At noon on the hotel's official opening day, the city is struck by a massive earthquake. Wright's hotel is one of the few buildings to survive.
1925	Walter and Marion Griffin move from Melbourne to Castlecrag in Australia.
1926	Pioneer Hi-Bred International in Iowa begins marketing hybrid seed corn.
1927	First Mason City airport is established. Charles Lindbergh attends the dedication.
1929	Griffin designs the Fishwick House in Castlecrag.
1930	William Van Alen designs the Chrysler Building in New York.
1935	Wright designs Fallingwater in rural Pennsylvania.
1935	Walter Burley Griffin leaves Castlecrag to work on architectural commissions in India, followed soon after by his wife, Marion.
1937	Following surgery, Walter Burley Griffin dies of peritonitis in India. Marion Mahony Griffin moves back to Castlecrag, then leaves Australia permanently in 1938. She returns to Chicago, where she remains for the rest of her life.
1939	Wright designs the Johnson Wax Building in Racine, Wisconsin.
1941	United States enters World War II.
1950	Television becomes a source of home entertainment.
1956	Wright designs the Guggenheim Museum in New York.
1959	Death of Frank Lloyd Wright.
1959	Former Wright apprentice Curtis Besinger designs the Tom MacNider House, a Usonian structure, in the Rock Crest/Rock Glen neighborhood in Mason City.
1962	Death of Marion Mahony Griffin.

1965	Opening of Charles H. MacNider Art Museum in Mason City.
1967	Death of Barry Byrne.
1992	Having been relocated in 1989 and restored to its historic state, Wright's Stockman House opens as a house museum.
2002	Opening of Music Man Square in Mason City.
2011	Its restoration complete, the Historic Park Inn Hotel opens in Mason City.
2011	Completion of the Robert E. McCoy Architectural Interpretive Center, adjacent to the Stockman House in Mason City.

NOTES

Introduction

1. Neutra, *Life and Shape.*
2. Ibid., 185.
3. Ibid., 181.
4. Ibid., 186.
5. Wilson and Robinson, *Prairie School in Iowa*, 10–16.
6. McCoy and Smith, *Mason City Walking Tour*, 53.
7. Schmitt et al., *Mason City, Iowa.*
8. Gebhard and Mansheim, *Buildings of Iowa.*
9. McCoy and Smith, *Mason City Walking Tour.*
10. Gebhard and Mansheim, *Buildings of Iowa.*
11. Sullivan, "Tall Office Building."
12. Behrens, "How Form Functions."
13. Bayley, *Conran Directory*, 6.
14. Ibid.

Chapter 1

15. Rooney, "World Series Earthquake," 17.
16. Secrest, *Frank Lloyd Wright*, 272.
17. West, "Japs Abolished," 5.
18. Behrens, "Merle Armitage."
19. McCoy, "Development and Developers," 20.
20. Ibid., 11.

21. Wright, "Fireproof House."
22. McCoy, "Development and Developers," 21.
23. McCoy and Smith, *Mason City Walking Tour*, 52.
24. Ibid., 53.
25. Secrest, *Frank Lloyd Wright*, 202–22.
26. Gill, *Many Masks*, 198–99.
27. Rodeghier, "Iowa's 'River City.'"
28. Gill, *Many Masks*, 204.
29. McCoy and Smith, *Mason City Walking Tour*, 26.
30. Alofsin, *Frank Lloyd Wright*, 137–40.
31. McCarter, *Frank Lloyd Wright*, 97.
32. Brosterman, *Inventing Kindergarten*.
33. Hubbard, *White Hyacinths*, 74.
34. Champney, *Art and Glory*, 1968.
35. Behrens, *False Colors*.
36. Brosterman, *Inventing Kindergarten*.
37. Ibid., 93.
38. Gill, *Many Masks*, 23.
39. Ibid., 25.
40. Secrest, *Frank Lloyd Wright*, 79.
41. McCoy, "Development and Developers," 5.
42. McCarter, *Frank Lloyd Wright*, 10.
43. McCoy, "Development and Developers," 5-6.
44. McCarter, *Frank Lloyd Wright*, 18.
45. Wright, *Autobiography*, 13.
46. Brosterman, *Inventing Kindergarten*.
47. Ibid., 84–87.
48. Fuller, *I Seem to Be a Verb*, 1.
49. Ibid.
50. Kaufmann and Raeburn, *Frank Lloyd Wright*, 19.
51. Ibid., 106.
52. James, *Principles of Psychology*, 1:350.
53. Brosterman, *Inventing Kindergarten*, 138.
54. Ibid., 46–48.
55. Wright, *Autobiography*, 16.
56. Thoreau, *Walden*, 224.
57. Meehan, *Master Architect*, 292.
58. Ibid., 307.
59. Ibid.
60. Alofsin, *Frank Lloyd Wright*, 11–12.
61. Wright, *Autobiography*.
62. Ibid.

63. Kruty, "Melding Architecture," 96.
64. Alofsin, *Frank Lloyd Wright*, 73–78.
65. Bayley, *Conran Directory*, 90–91.
66. Ibid., 191.
67. Ibid., 236.
68. Alofsin, *Frank Lloyd Wright*, 35–40.
69. Ibid.
70. Ibid., 12–16.
71. Kuty, "Melding Architecture," 80–85.
72. Gill, *Many Masks*, 198–09.
73. Ibid., 179–80.
74. Quoted in Haun, *Historic Park Inn Hotel*, 23.
75. Hurley, "Poetic Spaces."
76. Wright, *Ausgefuhrte*.
77. Nute, *Wright and Japan*, 80.
78. Quoted in Terkel, *Division Street*, 286.
79. Wright, *Ausgefuhrte*.
80. Stern, *Against Fashion*, 13; Hurley, "Poetic Spaces."
81. Stern, *Against Fashion*, 11–22.
82. Ibid., 13.
83. Fischer, *Klimt and Flöge*; Stern, *Against Fashion*, 23–28.
84. Hanks, *Decorative Designs*, 24–26; Stern, *Against Fashion*, 13.
85. Kaufmann and Raeburnm, *Frank Lloyd Wright*, 49.
86. Ibid.
87. Ibid.
88. Secrest, *Frank Lloyd Wright*, 217–22.
89. Gill, *Many Masks*, 229–34.
90. Ibid., 232.
91. Ibid., 229.

Chapter 2

92. Sage, *History of Iowa*.
93. Kantor, *Spirit Lake*.
94. McKean, "Joseph Paxton."
95. Ibid.
96. Ibid.
97. Bayley, *Conran Directory*, 166.
98. Jones, *Grammar of Ornament*.
99. Ibid., 5–8.
100. McCarter, *Frank Lloyd Wright*, 34.

101. Jones, *Grammar of Ornament*, 5.
102. Kaufmann and Raeburn, *Frank Lloyd Wright*, 296–97.
103. Tafel, *About Wright*, 91.
104. Kaufmann and Raeburn, *Frank Lloyd Wright*, 75.
105. Ibid., 104.
106. Hoffmann, *Frank Lloyd Wright*, 18.
107. Sigur, *Influence of Japanese Art*.
108. Nute, *Frank Lloyd Wright*, 11ff.
109. Ibid., 13.
110. Ibid., 21.
111. Meech, *Frank Lloyd Wright*, 21.
112. Dow, *Composition*.
113. Okakura, *Book of Tea*.
114. Dow, *Composition*, 103.
115. Quoted in Nute, *Frank Lloyd Wright*, 95.
116. Behrens, "How Form Functions" and *False Colors*.
117. Le Corbusier, *Towards a New Architecture*.
118. Hale, *Old Way of Seeing*, 47.
119. Ibid., 56.
120. Quoted in Hanks, *Decorative Designs*, 80.
121. Ibid., 54.
122. Introduction to Dow, *Composition*, 28.
123. Nute, *Frank Lloyd Wright*, 22–23.
124. Manson, *Frank Lloyd Wright*, 15–21.
125. Nute, *Frank Lloyd Wright*.
126. Ibid., 3.
127. Ibid.
128. Ibid., 4.
129. McCoy, "Development and Developers," 2.
130. Ibid., 4.
131. Ibid., 3.
132. Ibid., 2–3.
133. Patterson, *Frank Lloyd Wright*, 177ff.
134. Johnson, *Concrete Adobe*.
135. Giedion, *Mechanization Takes Command*, 213ff.
136. McCoy, "Development and Developers," 3–4.
137. *Facts About Sugar*, "Mason City's New Plant."
138. Ibid.
139. *Mason City Globe Gazette*, "W.H. Baird."
140. McCoy, "Development and Developers," 4.
141. See Giedion, *Mechanization Takes Command*.
142. McCoy, "Development and Developers," 4.

Chapter 3

143. Brooks, *Prairie School Architecture*, xii–xiii.
144. Wright, "City National Bank."
145. McCoy and Smith, *Mason City Walking Tour*, 9.
146. McCoy, "Rock Crest/Rock Glen," 11.
147. McCoy and Smith, *Mason City Walking Tour*, 2.
148. Sage, *History of Iowa*, 154.
149. McCoy and Smith, *Mason City Walking Tour*, 13.
150. Willson, *But He Doesn't Know.*
151. McCoy and Smith, *Mason City Walking Tour*, 13.
152. Associated Press, "Iowa Crash."
153. McCoy, "Development and Developers," 30–31.
154. McCoy and Smith, *Mason City Walking Tour*, 5.
155. Buehner, "Plenty of Folks."
156. Brosterman, *Inventing Kindergarten*, 46ff.
157. Patterson, *Frank Lloyd Wright*, 98–99.
158. Wright, "City National Bank."
159. Ibid.
160. Ibid.
161. Haun, *Historic Park Inn Hotel*, 17.
162. Ibid., 19.
163. Ibid., 18.
164. Schultz, Thomas and Borcherding, *Wright Again*, 21.
165. Haun, *Historic Park Inn Hotel*, 2007.
166. Sage, *History of Iowa*, 254.
167. Haun, *Historic Park Inn Hotel*, 29ff.
168. Ibid., 37ff.
169. Ibid., 37–38.
170. Ibid., 40.
171. Ibid., 44.
172. Ibid.
173. McCarter, *Frank Lloyd Wright*, 37.
174. Ibid.
175. Haun, *Historic Park Inn Hotel*, 45.
176. Schultz, Thomas and Borcherding, *Wright Again*, 2012.

Chapter 4

177. McCoy, "Development and Developers," 38ff.
178. Ibid.

179. Bang, *Melson House Revealed*, 7–9.
180. Kruty, "Melding Architecture," 42.
181. Ibid.
182. McCoy, "Development and Developers," 21.
183. Neutra, *Life and Shape*, 179–80.
184. McCoy and Smith, *Mason City Walking Tour*, 26.
185. Kruty, "Melding Architecture," 43.
186. Ibid., 44.
187. Ibid., 40–41.
188. Ibid.
189. Birmingham, "'I See Dead People.'"
190. McGregor, *Grand Obsessions*, 167.
191. Van Zanten, *Marion Mahoney Reconsidered*, 38.
192. Maldre and Kruty, *Walter Burley Griffin*, 33.
193. Twombly, *Prairie School*, 170.
194. Maldre and Kruty, *Walter Burley Griffin*, 20.
195. Kruty, "Melding Architecture," 44.
196. Mahony Griffin, "Magic of America."
197. Kruty, "Melding Architecture," 45.
198. Ibid., 46.
199. McGregor, *Grand Obsessions*, 159.
200. Kruty, "Melding Architecture," 46.
201. Ibid., 69ff.
202. McCoy and Smith, *Mason City Walking Tour*, 59.
203. Ibid., 57.
204. Brooks, *Prairie School*, 256.
205. Kruty, "Melding Architecture," 71.
206. Ibid., 74ff.
207. Ibid., 74–75.
208. Ibid., 55.
209. Ibid., 82.
210. Ibid., 80ff.
211. Haun, *Historic Park Inn Hotel*, 40.
212. Kruty, "Melding Architecture," 83.
213. McCoy and Smith, *Mason City Walking Tour*, 20.
214. Ibid., 30.
215. Kruty, "Melding Architecture," 85.
216. Gebhard and Mansheim, *Buildings of Iowa*, 413,
217. Kruty, "Melding Architecture," 85.
218. *Fergus Falls (MN) Daily Journal*, "Body of Local Man."
219. Haun, *Historic Park Inn Hotel*.
220. Kruty, "Melding Architecture," 59ff.

221. McCoy and Smith, *Mason City Walking Tour*, 58.
222. Brooks, *Prairie School*, 244.
223. Hurley, "Poetic Spaces," 64.
224. Bang, *Melson House Revealed*, 14.
225. Ibid., 18.
226. Ibid.
227. Weirick, "The New—," 52.
228. Ibid.
229. Gripper, "Angels in the Architecture.
230. Quoted in *New York Times*, Sunday, June 2, 1912.
231. Wright, *Autobiography*, 168.
232. Birmingham, "'I See Dead People,'" 144.
233. Terkel, *Division Street*, 249.
234. Scan of the message side of a handwritten postcard (dated 1941) to Markley from Frank Lloyd Wright, https://www.bonhams.com/auctions/22407/lot/84.

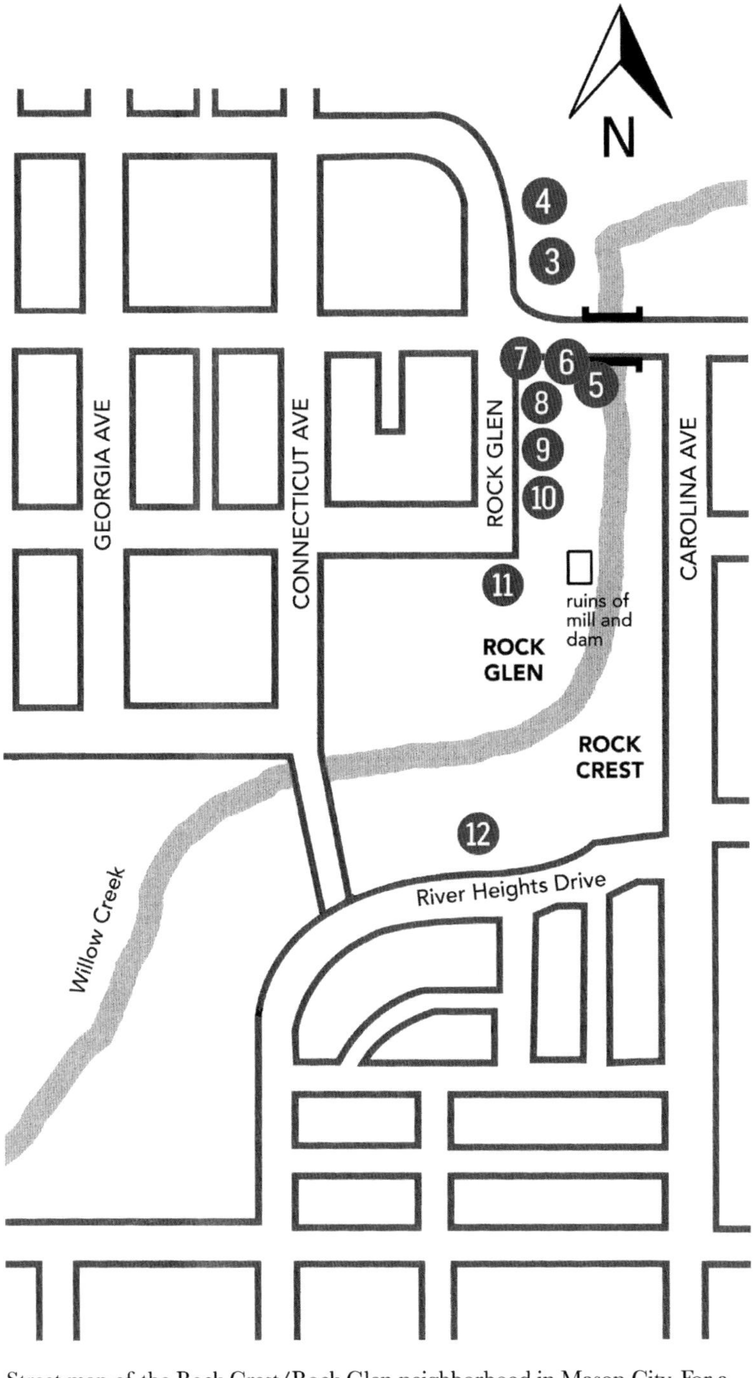

Street map of the Rock Crest/Rock Glen neighborhood in Mason City. For a full annotated street map, see page 113. *Author's diagram.*

BIBLIOGRAPHY

Alofsin, Anthony. *Frank Lloyd Wright: The Lost Years, 1910–1922*. Chicago: University of Chicago Press, 1993.

Associated Press. "Iowa Crash Kills 3 Singers; Rock 'n' Roll Stars and Pilot Die as Chartered Craft Falls After Its Take-Off." *New York Times*, February 3, 1959, 1.

Bang, Peggy L. *The Melson House Revealed: An Owner's Perspective*. Mason City, IA, 2015.

Banham, Reynar. *Theory and Design in the First Machine Age*. Cambridge, MA: MIT Press, 1980.

Bayley, Stephen, ed. *The Conran Directory of Design*. New York: Villard, 1985.

Behrens, Roy R. "Art, Design and Gestalt Theory." *Leonardo* 31 (1998): 299–303.

. "Elbert Hubbard, Dard Hunter and the Roycroft Workshops." *Ballast Quarterly Review* 17, no. 1 (Fall 2001).

———. *False Colors: Art, Design and Modern Camouflage*. Dysart, IA: Bobolink Books, 2002.

———. "How Form Functions: On Esthetics and Gestalt Theory." *Gestalt Theory* 24 (2002): 317–25.

———. "Merle Armitage: The Impresario of Book Design." *Ballast Quarterly Review* 16, no. 3 (Summer 2001).

Birmingham, Elizabeth. "'I See Dead People': Archive, Crypt, and an Argument for the Researcher's Sixth Sense." In *Beyond the Archives: Research as a Lived Process*, edited by Gesa Kirsch and Liz Rohan, 139–46. Carbondale: University of Southern Illinois Press, 2008.

Brooks, H. Allen. *The Prairie School: Frank Lloyd Wright and His Midwest Contemporaries*. New York: W.W. Norton, 1976.

———, ed. *Prairie School Architecture: Studies from The Western Architect*. Toronto: University of Toronto Press, 1975.

———, ed. *Writings on Wright: Selected Comment on Frank Lloyd Wright.* Cambridge, MA: MIT Press, 1981.

Brosterman, Norman. *Inventing Kindergarten.* New York: Abrams, 1997.

Buehner, Kristin. "Plenty of Folks Still Remember Infamous Dillinger Bank Robbery." *Mason City Globe Gazette*, September 19, 2008.

Champney, Freeman. *Art and Glory: The Story of Elbert Hubbard.* New York: Crown Publishers, 1968.

Dow, Arthur W. *Composition: A Series of Exercises in Art Structure for the Use of Students and Teachers.* Reprint ed. Berkeley: University of California Press, 1997.

Facts About Sugar. "Mason City's New Plant to be Efficiency Model." October 14, 1916, 230.

Fergus Falls (MN) Daily Journal. "Body of Local Man is Found in River." April 16, 1948.

Fischer, Wolfgang G. *Gustav Klimt and Emilie Flöge: An Artist and His Muse.* Woodstock, NY: Overlook Press, 1992.

Fuller, R. Buckminster. *I Seem to Be a Verb.* New York: Bantam Books, 1970.

Gebhard, David, and Gerald Mansheim. *Buildings of Iowa.* New York: Oxford University Press, 1993.

Giedion, Siegfried. *Mechanization Takes Command: A Contribution to Anonymous History.* Oxford, UK: Oxford University Press, 1948.

Gill, Brendan. *Many Masks: A Life of Frank Lloyd Wright.* New York: Ballantine Books, 1987.

Griffin, Walter B. "Rock Crest and Rock Glen. Domestic Community Development, Mason City, Iowa." *Western Architect* 19 (1913): 75–76.

Gripper, Ali. "Angels in the Architecture." *Sydney Morning Herald*, June 30, 2000, 69.

Hale, Jonathan. *The Old Way of Seeing.* Boston: Houghton Mifflin, 1994.

Hanks, David A. *The Decorative Designs of Frank Lloyd Wright.* New York: E.P. Dutton, 1979.

Haun, Katherine. *The Historic Park Inn Hotel and City National Bank.* Revised and edited by Pat Schultz. Mason City, IA: Wright on the Park, 2010.

Hoffmann, Donald. *Frank Lloyd Wright: Architecture and Nature.* New York: Dover, 1986.

Hubbard, Elbert. *White Hyacinths.* East Aurora, New York: Roycroft Press, 1907.

Hurley, C.J. "Poetic Spaces: Designing Gesamtkunstwerk, the 'Total Work of Art.'" *Style 1900 Magazine* (Spring 2010): 56–65.

James, William. *The Principles of Psychology.* 2 vols. New York: Henry Holt, 1890.

Johnson, Donald Leslie. *Frank Lloyd Wright's Concrete Adobe: Irving Gill, Rudolph Schindler and the American Southwest.* Farnham, Surry, UK: Ashgate Publishing, 2013.

Jones, Owen. *The Grammar of Ornament.* London: Bernard Quaritch, 1910.

Kantor, MacKinlay. *Spirit Lake.* New York: World Publishing, 1961.

Kaufmann, Edgar, and Ben Raeburn, eds. *Frank Lloyd Wright: Writings and Buildings*. New York: Meridian Books, 1960.

Kruty, Paul. "Melding Architecture to Landscape in North-Central Iowa." In *Rock Crest/Rock Glen, Mason City, Iowa: The American Masterwork of Marion M. and Walter B. Griffin*, edited by Kruty et al., 35–96. St. Louis, MO: Walter Burley Griffin Society of America, 2014.

Kruty, Paul, Robert E. McCoy, Paul E. Sprague and James Weirick. *Rock Crest/ Rock Glen, Mason City, Iowa: The American Masterwork of Marion M. and Walter B. Griffin*. St. Louis, MO: Walter Burley Griffin Society of America, 2014.

Le Corbusier, Frederick Etchells. *Towards a New Architecture*. 1927. Reprint, London: Architectural Press, 2014.

Lind, Carla. *The Wright Style*. New York: Simon and Schuster, 1992.

Mahony Griffin, Marion. "The Magic of America." Unpublished typescript, 1940–49.

Maldre, Mati, and Paul Kruty. *Walter Burley Griffin in America*. Urbana: University of Illinois Press, 1996.

Manning, Richard. *Grassland: The History, Biology, Politics and Promise of the American Prairie*. New York: Penguin, 1995.

Manson, Grant C. *Frank Lloyd Wright to 1910: The First Golden Age*. New York: Reinhold Publishing, 1958.

Mason City Globe Gazette. "W.H. Baird, Builder of Sugar Factories, Dies." January 7, 1933, 1.

McCarter, Robert. *Frank Lloyd Wright*. London: Phaidon, 1997.

McCoy, Robert E. "The Development and Developers of Rock Crest / Rock Glen." In *Rock Crest/Rock Glen, Mason City, Iowa: The American Masterwork of Marion M. and Walter B. Griffin*, edited by Kruty et al., 1–32. St. Louis, MO: Walter Burley Griffin Society of America, 2014.

———. "Rock Crest / Rock Glen: Prairie School Planning in Iowa." *Prairie School Review* 5 (1968): 5–39.

McCoy, Robert E., and Jim Smith, eds. *Mason City Walking Tour*. Mason City, IA: River City Society for Historic Preservation, 2012.

McGregor, Alasdair. *Grand Obsessions: The Life and Work of Walter Burley Griffin and Marion Mahony Griffin*. Camberwell, VIC: Penguin Books, 2009.

McKean, John. "Joseph Paxton: Crystal Palace, London 1851." In *Lost Masterpieces* (Architecture 3s Series). London: Phaidon Press, unpaged, 1999.

Meech, Julia. *Frank Lloyd Wright and the Art of Japan: The Architect's Other Passion*. New York: Abrams, 2001.

Meehan, Patrick J., ed. *The Master Architect: Conversations with Frank Lloyd Wright*. New York: John Wiley, 1984.

Mitchell, W.O. *Who Has Seen the Wind*. Boston: Little, Brown, 1947.

Neutra, Richard. *Life and Shape*. New York: Appleton-Century-Crofts, 1962.

Nute, Kevin. *Frank Lloyd Wright and Japan*. New York: Van Nostrand Reinhold, 1993.

Okakura, Kakuzo. *The Book of Tea*. London: Putnam's Sons, 1906.

Patterson, Terry L. *Frank Lloyd Wright and the Meaning of Materials*. New York: Van Nostrand Reinhold, 1994.

Pregliasco, Janice. "The Life and Work of Marion Mahony Griffin." *Art Institute of Chicago Museum Studies* 21 (1995): 64–181ff.

Rodeghier, Katherine. "Iowa's 'River City' a Trove of Prairie School Architecture." *Chicago Tribune*, March 19, 2015.

Rooney, Andy. "World Series Earthquake." *The Hour*, October 23, 1989.

Sage, Leland. *A History of Iowa*. Ames: Iowa State University Press, 1974.

Schmitt, Ronald E., et al. *Mason City, Iowa, an Architectural Heritage: An Inventory of Historic and Architecturally Significant Buildings*. Mason City, IA: Department of Community Development, 1977.

Schrag, Peter. "Is Main Street Still There?" *Saturday Review*, January 17, 1970, 20–25.

Schultz, Pat, Dana Thomas and Scott Borcherding. *Wright Again: Transforming Frank Lloyd Wright's City National Bank and Hotel into the Historic Park Inn Hotel*. Mason City, IA: Wright on the Park, 2012.

Scully, Vincent. *Frank Lloyd Wright.* New York: George Braziller, 1960.

Secrest, Meryle. *Frank Lloyd Wright*. New York: Knopf, 1992.

Sigur, Hannah. *The Influence of Japanese Art on Design*. Layton, Utah: Gibbs Smith, 2008.

Sprague, Paul E. "Griffin's Architecture in Mason City." In *Rock Crest/Rock Glen, Mason City, Iowa: The American Masterwork of Marion M. and Walter B. Griffin*, edited by Kruty et al., 97–146. St. Louis, MO: Walter Burley Griffin Society of America, 2014.

Stern, Radu. *Against Fashion: Clothing as Art, 1850–1930*. Cambridge, MA: MIT Press, 2004.

Sullivan, Louis H. "The Tall Office Building Artistically Considered," *Lippincott's Magazine* (March 1896): 403–09.

Tafel, Edgar. *About Wright: An Album of Recollections by Those Who Knew Frank Lloyd Wright*. New York: John Wiley, 1993.

———. *Apprentice to Genius: Years with Frank Lloyd Wright*. New York: McGraw-Hill, 1979.

Terkel, Studs. *Division Street*. Berkeley: University of California Press, 1967.

Thoreau, Henry D. *Thoreau's Walden*. New York: Longmans, Green and Company, 1910.

Twombly, Robert C. *The Prairie School: Design Vision for the Midwest*. Chicago: Art Institute of Chicago, 1995.

Van Zanten, David, ed. *Marion Mahony Reconsidered*. Chicago: University of Chicago Press, 2000.

Weirick, James. 2014. "The New—and the Primal Past: From Mason City, Iowa to Middle Harbor, Sydney." In *Rock Crest/Rock Glen, Mason City, Iowa: The American Masterwork of Marion M. and Walter B. Griffin*, edited by Kruty et al., 147–158. St. Louis, MO: Walter Burley Griffin Society of America, 2014.

West, Irene. "Japs Abolished Rickshaw Coolies." *Afro American*, February 17, 1945, 5.

Willson, Meredith. *But He Doesn't Know the Territory*. Minneapolis: University of Minnesota Press, 2009.

Wilson, Robert Guy, and Sidney K. Robinson. *The Prairie School in Iowa*. Ames: Iowa State University Press, 1977.

Wright, Frank Lloyd. *Ausgefuhrte Bauten und Entwurfe von Frank Lloyd Wright*. Berlin: Wasmuth, 1910. Reprint, *Drawings and Plans of Frank Lloyd Wright*. New York: Dover, 1983.

———. "City National Bank of Mason City, Iowa, Frank Lloyd Wright, Architect." *Western Architect* 19 (December 1911).

———. "A Fireproof House for $5000." *Ladies' Home Journal* 24 (April 1907): 24.

———. *Frank Lloyd Wright: An Autobiography*. Petaluma, CA: Pomegranate Communications, 2005.

Other Sources

Gift shop: Wright on the Park Headquarters/Gift Shop, 17 South Federal Avenue; (641) 423-0689; http://www.wrightonthepark.org

Historic Park Inn: 7 West State Street; (641) 422-0015, (800) 659-2220; http://www.stoneycreekhotels.com/hotel/travel/masoncity-parkinn/home.do

Hotel tours: Wright on the Park guided tours of Historic Park Inn; (641) 423-0689; http://www.wrightonthepark.org

Mason City Public Library: 225 Second Street Southeast. See especially the Archives and History Department at http://www.mcpl.org/historyandgenealogy.

Robert L. McCoy Architectural Interpretive Center (adjacent to the Stockman House): 520 First Street Northeast; (641) 423-1923; http://www.stockmanhouse.org

Stockman House tours: 530 First Street Northeast; (641) 423-1923; http://www.stockmanhouse.org

Visitor info: (800) 423-5724; http://www.VisitMasonCityIowa.com

ABOUT THE AUTHOR

Roy R. Behrens is professor of art and distinguished scholar at the University of Northern Iowa. He has taught graphic design and design history at American art schools, colleges and universities for nearly forty-five years and has lectured internationally.

The author of eight books and hundreds of academic journal and magazine articles, he is especially known for his writings about art, design and camouflage. He has been featured in interviews on NOVA, National Public Radio, Australian Public Radio, BBC, Iowa Public Radio and Iowa Public Television, as well as in documentary films.

Described by *Communication Arts* magazine as "one of the most original thinkers in design," he was a nominee for the Smithsonian Institution's National Design Awards in 2003.